Triton BOATS

OUTDOORSMAN'S COOKBOOK

Benefiting DELTA WATERFOWL

[*Edited by Craig Lamb*]

[interactive blvd.]™

An Interactive Blvd.™ Book
www.InteractiveBlvd.com

Published by Interactive Blvd.™, a division of 4964 Productions, LLC,
121 21st Avenue North, Suite 305, Nashville, Tennessee 37203

Graphic Design by Creative Access, Inc., Nashville, Tennessee
Food Photography by Ed Rode
Other Photography courtesy of Triton Boats, Delta Waterfowl, Bombardier and Team Triton Pros
All recipes except those attributed to Team Triton Pros are from *The Great Outdoorsman Cookbook* ©2003 by Jimmy Holt and Vernon Summerlin and used by permission of Rutledge Hill Press, Nashville, Tennessee.

Library of Congress Control number: 2003115823

TABLE OF CONTENTS

INTRODUCTION

By Roland Martin
Bass fishing's most legendary angler

To fully enjoy the great outdoors means to experience it firsthand and take home some of its bountiful offerings to the dinner table. As any avid outdoorsman knows, cooking wild game and fish are on an equal scale of gratification with the pursuit of the quarry.

And those fundamental principles of fishing and hunting are the essence of the *Triton Boats Outdoorsman's Cookbook*. Yet to call this a cookbook in the true sense of the word is open for debate. You can ultimately decide where the book spends idle time: on the bookshelf with other favorite outdoor reads, or ready for use in the kitchen.

In theory this is a cookbook. In addition to some tried-and-true favorites, many of the recipes have been contributed by famous outdoorsmen who just happen to be excellent cooks. Some are considered legends, others are champions of their trade, and all spend countless days afield or on the water perfecting their skills.

The lifelong experiences of these exemplary outdoorsmen are found throughout the pages of this book in the form of recipes and helpful tips. In a sense, reading this book is like being invited to dinner at their camp or home. You enjoy food, fellowship and likely return home with a great recipe from their kitchen along with enlightenment on how to improve your enjoyment of the outdoors.

Fishermen and hunters are the conservation leaders of our great nation. And that makes fishing and hunting a viable part of fish and wildlife management. Outdoorsmen spend millions of dollars annually on fishing and hunting licenses with the fees collectively distributed by the federal government back to states for conservation of our natural resources. Many outdoorsmen go above and beyond the call of conservation by supporting organizations whose mission is to further preserve the legacy of fishing and hunting for future generations.

Among that group is the growing membership of the Delta Waterfowl Foundation, an organization whose avid waterfowlers are committed to funding and supporting research efforts to improve wetlands across North America. Delta Waterfowl's agenda is focused first and foremost on wetlands because these fragile and complex ecosystems are endangered by rampant development from urban sprawl and pollution. This campaign to save wetlands means protecting drinking water supplies and the only remaining wilderness areas in the nation.

As you flip through the pages of this book I imagine you will begin to feel a growl in your stomach as the delicacies begin to stir your appetite. And, if you are like me, reading the yarns and tips from the contributors will make your mind wander into the great outdoors.

If that is the case, then enjoy your outdoor memories and the bounty of game and fish that can only come from a fishing or hunting trip.

Enjoy.

Roland Martin

ROLAND MARTIN'S professional bass fishing career spans more than three decades and counting. This bass fishing great has won an unprecedented 19 BASS championships and nine point titles. Martin is recognized as one of the most innovative anglers on the pro tour for his ingenious strategies and fishing inventions. He is also the host of *Fishing with Roland Martin* on cable's Outdoor Life Network.

His infatuation for catching anything that swims is matched by an equal passion for hunting wild turkey, deer and other game species.

THE BASICS

The reward of cooking fish and game isn't just telling the story of how you delivered the dish from the outdoors to the dinner table. Moreover, you can impress yourself and dinner guests by experimenting with recipes in the kitchen and turning out a delicious dish.

But before you try to swap a seasoning, or create your own marinade, there are a few basics you should know. An ounce of one ingredient isn't always the same as an ounce of another.

The charts and tips in this chapter will give you the information you need to enjoy cooking not only the recipes in this book, but to mix-and-match them to create some recipes of your own.

Conversion Charts

DRY

1/4 cup = 4 Tablespoons
1/3 cup = 5 Tablespoons + 1 teaspoon
1/2 cup = 8 Tablespoons or 4 oz.
3/4 cup = 12 Tablespoons
1 cup = 16 Tablespoons
1 cup = 48 teaspoons
2 cups = 1 pint
4 cups = 1 quart
1 oz. = 1/16 pound
2 oz. = 1/8 pound
3 oz. = 3/16 pound
4 oz. = 1/4 pound
8 oz. = 1/2 pound
12 oz. = 3/4 pound
16 oz. = 1 pound
32 oz. = 2 pounds
1 kilogram = 2.2 pounds or 35.2 oz.

LIQUID

1/2 Tablespoon = 1 1/2 teaspoons
1 Tablespoon = 3 teaspoons
2 Tablespoon = 1 fluid oz.
1/4 cup = 2 fluid oz. or 4 Tablespoons
1/3 cup = 2 2/3 fluid oz. or 5 Tablespoons + 1 teaspoon
1/2 cup = 4 fluid oz. or 8 Tablespoons
2/3 cup = 5 1/3 fluid oz. or 10 Tablespoons + 2 teaspoons
3/4 cup = 6 fluid oz. or 12 Tablespoons
7/8 cup = 7 fluid oz. or 14 Tablespoons
1 cup = 8 fluid oz. or 16 Tablespoons
2 cups = 16 fluid oz. or 1 pint
2 pints = 32 fluid oz. or 1 quart
4 quarts = 1 gallon

FOOD

1 stick butter = 8 Tablespoons butter
1 pound butter = 4 sticks butter
1/2 pound hard cheese = approximately 2 cups grated cheese
1 pound apples = approximately 3 apples
1 medium lemon = approximately 3 Tablespoons lemon juice
or 2 or 3 teaspoons grated peel
1 large onion = approximately 1 cup chopped onion
1 cup raw converted rice = 4 cups cooked rice
1 large tomato = approximately 3/4 cup chopped tomato
1 pound all purpose flour = approximately 4 cups sifted flour
2 slices bread = 1 cup fresh breadcrumbs

BAKING

1 cup sifted cake flour = 1 cup - 2 Tablespoons sifted all purpose flour
1 cup sifted all purpose flour = 1 cup + 2 Tablespoons sifted cake flour
1 teaspoon double-acting baking powder = 1/4 teaspoon baking soda + 1/2 teaspoon cream of tartar

METRIC CONVERSION FACTORS

1 fluid oz. = 29.6 milliliters
1 U.S. pint = 0.473 liter
1 U.S. quart = 0.946 liter
1 U.S. gallon = 0.84 imperial gallon = 3.8 liters
1 imperial gallon = 1.2 U.S. gallons = 4.5 liters
1 dry pint = 0.55 liters
1 dry quart = 1.1 liters
1 cubic centimeter = 0.06 cubic inch
1 cubic centimeter = 0.06 cubic inch
1 milliliter = 0.034 fluid ounce
1 liter = 1.06 U.S.quarts = 0.9 dry quart

METRIC UNITS

1 cubic centimeter (cc) = 1/1,000,000 cubic meter
1 cubic decimeter (cu dm) = 1/1,000 cubic meter
= 1,000 cubic decimeters
1 cubic meter (cu m) = 1 stere (s)
1 milliliter (ml) = 1/1,0000 liter
= 1 cubic centimeter
1 centiliter (cl) = 1/100 liter = 10 milliliters
1 deciliter (dl) = 1/10 liter
1 liter = 1 cubic decimeter

MISCELLANEOUS

1 cup stock = 1 bouillon cube dissolved in 1 cup of boiling water
1 oz. of baking unsweetened chocolate = 3 Tablespoons cocoa powder + 1 Tablespoon butter
1 oz. semisweet chocolate = 3 Tablespoons cocoa powder + 2 Tablespoons butter + 3 Tablespoons sugar
1 Tablespoon prepared mustard = 1 teaspoon dried mustard

Over the years of hunting, fishing and cooking, the Team Triton pros have learned a few tips to help make life a little easier when preparing their kill for the table. Follow these hints in the field and in the kitchen and you'll find preparing your meal can be as fun as catching it.

- Clean fish as soon as you can and place the fresh fillets on ice, if state or federal regulations allow separating meat from the carcass before you leave the lake.

- Depending on the law, do the same thing with wild game: Clean it and allow the meat to cool and then ice it down for the trip home.

- A sharp knife is a fundamental tool for preparing game and fish in the field. Nothing is worse than a dull knife, which can destroy a prime cut of meat.

- If you keep other parts of the animal for other purposes, separate them from the carcass as soon as possible and store them inside individual freezer bags on ice.

- Have an idea ahead of time about what general recipes you might prepare with your catch or harvest. This will give you a better idea how to clean and carve specific cuts of meat like fillets, roasts and steaks.

- Before you start cooking, read the recipe all the way through so you know what comes when and how long each step takes. Then gather all of your ingredients and prep them before you start cooking. This way you'll have what you need when you need it, and you won't run into any surprises.

- To peel a tomato, drop it in a pot of boiling water for about 20 seconds and then put it under cold water. Then, with a sharp knife, cut two slits, crosswise, at the stem end and peel the skin away. It should come off easily; if it doesn't repeat the hot/cold process for about 10 seconds more and you should be in good shape.

- To peel a clove of garlic simply place it on a flat surface and hit it with the flat edge of a chef's or other large knife and press down. That will loosen the "paper" casing and you can slide the clove right out.

- Before frying breaded foods, let them stand at room temperature for about 20 minutes so the coating will stick better.
- When measuring liquids, always leave the measuring cup on the counter and bend down to see how much you've poured. When you bring the measuring cup up to eye level you'll end up holding it at an angle - no matter how hard you try - and you won't actually have the amount you think you have.
- When measuring flour (or similar ingredients) always spoon the flour into the measuring cup. Don't use the measuring cup as a scoop; this packs the flour into the cup too much and you'll get more than you want.
- The only ingredient you ever want to pack when measuring is brown sugar.
- Always preheat your oven and let it run through a cycle before putting your dish in. And don't keep opening the door to see if it's done; all that does is let hot air out and lower the oven temperature. Use your oven light or wait until you're pretty certain it's ready.

ENTREES

ARROW PLACEMENT *by Gary Klein*

The single most important thing when hunting with a bow and arrow is arrow placement. Whether you are shooting a long bow, recurve or a high tech cam bow, success still boils down to arrow placement. Practice! Know your equipment! Shoot as often as you can.

CROCK-POT VENISON STEW

2 pounds venison stew meat

2 Tablespoons butter

Salt and pepper

1/4 cup onion, chopped

2 teaspoons garlic powder

1/4 cup water

1/4 cup red wine

1 (8 oz.) can tomato sauce

3 potatoes, peeled and sliced

3 carrots, peeled and sliced

Place all ingredients in a Crock-Pot and stir to combine. Cook 8 to 10 hours on high.

PREP TIME: 20 minutes | **COOK TIME:** 8 to 10 hours | **SERVES:** 6 to 8

VENISON PEPPER STEAK

submitted by DAVID HALE

1 pound deer steak, cut 1/4" thick

Salt water

2 Tablespoons fat

1/4 cup onion, chopped

1 garlic clove, minced

1 bell pepper, cut in thin strips or rings

1 teaspoon salt

Dash of pepper

1 cube beef bouillon

1 cup hot water

2 Tablespoons soy sauce

2 Tablespoons cornstarch

1/4 cup cold water

1 pound tomatoes, chopped (optional)

Soak the deer in salt water for 8 to 12 hours in the refrigerator.

Rinse, cut meat in finger-size pieces and brown in fat. Add the onion, garlic and bell pepper. Season with the salt and pepper. Dissolve the bouillon cube in the hot water and add to meat. Cover and simmer until the meat is tender, 20 to 25 minutes. Combine the soy sauce, cornstarch and cold water, and stir into the meat mixture. Simmer until the gravy thickens. Remove the garlic. One pound of tomatoes can be added at the same time as the cornstarch mixture. Serve over hot noodles or mashed potatoes and homemade biscuits.

MARINATE: 8-12 HOURS | PREP TIME: 20 minutes | COOK TIME: 45 minutes | SERVES: 4

VENISON STEW

1 pound venison, cubed

1 (15 oz.) can crushed tomatoes, or freshly grown tomatoes, chopped

1 large onion, chopped

2 or 3 celery ribs, chopped

2 large potatoes, peeled and sliced

3 carrots, scraped and sliced

2 teaspoons instant bouillon

1/4 cup water

1/4 cup parsley, chopped

1/4 cup wine (optional)

Salt and pepper

Place the venison, tomatoes, onion, celery, potatoes, carrots, bouillon, water, parsley and wine in a large Dutch oven or pot. Cook for 1 hour over medium heat. Lower heat and simmer for 6 to 8 hours. Season with salt and pepper to taste.

PREP TIME: 30 minutes | **COOK TIME:** 7 to 9 hours | **SERVES:** 4 to 6

STUFFED GRAPE LEAVES

12 large grape leaves

Water

1/4 pound ground venison

1 medium onion, minced

2 Tablespoons vegetable oil

1 teaspoon grated lemon peel

1 teaspoon salt

1/4 teaspoon pepper

1/4 cup white raisins

2 cups cooked rice

1 cup water

Preheat the oven to 350°.

Grease a 1 1/2-quart casserole. Wash grape leaves. Blanch the grape leaves in boiling water for 30 seconds. Drain leaves, plunge in cold water, drain again and set aside. In a large skillet, brown the ground venison and onion in oil. Stir in the lemon peel, salt, pepper, raisins and rice. Place 1/3 cup of filling on each leaf. Fold the leaves around the filling. Place in the casserole with folded sides down. Add water, cover and bake for 20 to 30 minutes, until the liquid is almost gone.

PREP TIME: 15 minutes | **COOK TIME:** 30 to 40 minutes | **SERVES:** 4

BARBECUED VENISON BURGERS

1 pound ground venison

1/4 cup oatmeal

1/4 teaspoon salt

1/4 teaspoon pepper

1/4 cup evaporated milk

Barbecue sauce (recipe follows)

Mix the venison, oatmeal, salt, pepper and evaporated milk. Let the meat mixture flavors blend while you prepare the barbecue sauce. Shape meat mixture into 4 patties. Brown them in a large iron skillet and add the sauce. Let simmer for 30 to 40 minutes.

Note:
This recipe also works well over a camp fire, or even in a Crock-Pot.

BARBECUE SAUCE

1 Tablespoon Worcestershire

1/4 Tablespoon vinegar

1 Tablespoon sugar

1/4 cup ketchup

1/4 cup water

1 medium onion, finely chopped

In a small bowl, mix the Worcestershire, vinegar, sugar, ketchup, water and onion.

PREP TIME: 20 minutes | **COOK TIME:** 45 to 50 minutes | **SERVES:** 4

BAKED TROUT IN SOUR CREAM

3 to 4 medium trout fillets

Butter or margarine

Salt and pepper

1 (6 oz.) container sour cream

Cooked white rice

Preheat the oven to 350°.

Arrange the fish in a shallow baking dish. Dot with butter or margarine. Sprinkle with salt and pepper to taste. Cover with a liberal amount of the sour cream. Bake in the oven for 50 to 60 minutes or until done. Serve with rice.

PREP TIME: 5 minutes | **COOK TIME:** 1 hour | **SERVES:** 2 to 4

VENISON CHILI

2 pounds ground venison

1/4 cup vegetable oil

1 cup onion, chopped

2 garlic cloves, minced

1 large green pepper, cut in strips

3 Tablespoons chili powder

2 teaspoons sugar

3 1/4 cups canned whole tomatoes

1 cup tomato sauce

1 cup water

1/4 teaspoon salt

1 Tablespoon all purpose flour (optional)

2 Tablespoons water (optional)

2 cups kidney beans

Mozzarella or cheddar cheese for topping (optional)

In a large iron skillet, brown the venison in the vegetable oil. Add the onions, garlic and green pepper. Cook 5 minutes, stirring constantly. Add the chili powder, sugar, tomatoes, tomato sauce, water and salt. If a thicker chili is desired, stir in the 1 Tablespoon flour mixed with 2 Tablespoons water. Cover and simmer for 15 minutes. Just before serving, add the beans. Top with grated mozzarella or cheddar cheese if desired.

PREP TIME: 15 minutes | **COOK TIME:** 30 minutes | **SERVES:** 6 to 8

CATCHING SNOOK *by Roland Martin*

Jerk baits or top water baits are your best bet if you are at the mouth of a small feeder creek on an outgoing tide. You'll also have better luck fishing for snook August through December when water temperatures are in the mid-70's. When the temperature outside starts to drop and water temperatures get below the low-70s the snook tend to shut down. Mangrove Creeks from Marco Island to Flamingo are the areas I recommend.

GRILLED SNOOK

submitted by **ROLAND MARTIN**

4 1" thick snook fillets
Italian dressing

Heat grill to steak-searing temperature. Place snook filet on grill.

Baste with zesty Italian dressing, 2 times per side. Flip filet after 2 minutes, cook other side 2 minutes and remove.

PREP TIME: 10 minutes | COOK TIME: 4 minutes | SERVES: 4

VENISON AND RICE CASSEROLE

1 onion, chopped

1 green pepper, chopped

1 1/4 pounds venison, cut in bite-size pieces

2 Tablespoons shortening

2 teaspoons salt

1 Tablespoon brown sugar

3 cups canned tomatoes, undrained

1 cup rice, uncooked

Preheat the oven to 325°.

Sauté the onion, green pepper and venison in the shortening in a skillet until browned. Add the salt, brown sugar, tomatoes and rice; mix well. Pour the venison mixture into a casserole and bake for 1 hour.

PREP TIME: 20 minutes | **COOK TIME:** 1 hour 15 minutes | **SERVES:** 6 to 8

BARBECUED VENISON ROAST

1 venison roast

Salt and pepper

All purpose flour

2 Tablespoons shortening

Barbecue sauce (recipe follows)

Rinse the venison roast in cool water. Sprinkle the roast with salt and pepper. Roll in the flour and brown in shortening in a large iron skillet. Turn the roast to brown on all sides. Put the roast in a large pot with a lid and cook on top of the stove until tender. Remove from the pot and let cool. Remove any excess fat and bone. Chop the meat. Add the barbecue sauce to the chopped meat and let simmer for 30 to 40 minutes. (This recipe also freezes well.)

BARBECUE SAUCE

1/4 cup vinegar

9 ounces Heinz® chili sauce

1 medium onion, chopped

2 Tablespoons sugar

One red pepper pod

Combine the vinegar, chili sauce, onion, sugar and red pepper. Mix well.

Note:

If you are in a hurry, you may follow the recipe using your favorite pre-made barbecue sauce.

PREP TIME: 15 minutes | **COOK TIME:** 50 minutes | **SERVES:** 6 to 8

HUNTING TIP *by David Hale*

Never call a deer from a treestand the deer can see beyond. If he doesn't see any other deer then he won't come to you. Place your stand next to a thicket when calling to make the deer wonder if there are others in there.

VENISON ROAST WITH MUSHROOMS

4 Tablespoons shortening
3 pounds boned and rolled venison roast
1 large onion, sliced
1 cup water
1 cup tomato juice
1 teaspoon salt
1 teaspoon black pepper
1 teaspoon sugar
1 bay leaf
2 bouillon cubes
4 (3 oz.) cans sliced mushrooms
1/4 cup red wine

Preheat the oven to 325°.

Heat the shortening in a roasting pan on top of the stove. Add the roast, brown on all sides, add the onion, and brown 5 minutes longer. Combine the water, tomato juice, salt, pepper and sugar, and pour over the meat. Remove from the heat. Add the bay leaf, bouillon cubes and mushrooms; cover. Bake at 325° for about 2 hours and 15 minutes. Add the wine and bake for 15 minutes longer.

PREP TIME: 10 minutes | **COOK TIME:** 2 1/2 hours | **SERVES:** 4 to 6

VENISON POT ROAST

3 to 5 pound venison roast

2 teaspoons salt

1/4 teaspoon black pepper

1/4 cup all purpose flour

3 Tablespoons shortening

4 to 6 small onions, chopped

1 cup water

Potatoes (optional)

Carrots (optional)

Season the venison with salt and pepper; dredge in the flour. In a large Dutch oven, brown the venison on all sides in hot shortening, adding the onions and water. Cover and simmer until tender, 2 to 3 hours. Potatoes and carrots may be added 20 to 30 minutes before the roast is done.

PREP TIME: 10 minutes | **COOK TIME:** 2 to 3 hours | **SERVES:** 6 to 10

GRILLED VENISON STEAKS

8 venison steaks

1 (10 oz.) bottle Worcestershire

1 (6 oz.) bottle steak sauce

1/3 cup lemon pepper

Garlic salt

1 1/2 onions, minced

Marinate the steaks overnight in the refrigerator in a mixture of the Worcestershire, steak sauce, lemon pepper, garlic salt and onions, turning occasionally.

Put the steaks on the grill over medium-hot coals and baste with remaining marinade until steaks reach desired doneness.

PREP TIME: 10 minutes | MARINATE: overnight | **COOK TIME:** 15 to 20 minutes | **SERVES:** 8

STEWED RABBIT

2 rabbits

Salt and pepper

2 medium onions, finely chopped

3 Tablespoons vegetable oil

1 ham, cut into 1" cubes

1 cup water

1 (8 oz.) can mushrooms

2 Tablespoons sherry

Clean the rabbits and cut at the joints into serving pieces. Rub each piece with salt and pepper. Brown the rabbit and onions in vegetable oil; then add the cubed ham, water, mushrooms and sherry. Stir well, and adjust seasoning to taste. Simmer 1 hour.

PREP TIME: 30 minutes | **COOK TIME:** 1 hour | **SERVES:** 6 to 8

KEN AND TAMMY COOK'S TARBONE BUZZARD BREATH CHILI

submitted by KEN COOK

1 pound deer or elk burger, no fat
2 pounds deer or elk steak, cubed
1 large onion, chopped
4 cloves garlic, chopped
2 cans diced tomatoes seasoned with pepper and onions in the can
1 (6 oz.) can tomato paste
2 cans tomato sauce
2 cans ranch style kidney beans
2 cans ranch style beans
Salt, pepper and Tony's® seasoning to taste
2 cans mushrooms
5 stalks celery, peeled and chopped
2 packages Lawry's® Texas-style chili mix
1 can Ro-Tel® original
1 bay leaf
Dash celery salt

Sauté the meat, onions and garlic in a large skillet or stewpot until venison is brown. Drain well. Combine remaining ingredients, including celery; mix well. Bring to a boil; reduce heat. Simmer for 1 to 2 hours (depending on how hungry you are), stirring occasionally.

Serve with crackers and homemade sweet pickles and plenty of iced tea.

PREP TIME: 20 minutes | **COOK TIME:** 2 hours and 30 minutes | **SERVES:** 6 to 8

VENISON STROGANOFF

1 pound venison steak

1 onion, chopped

Vegetable oil

1 (10 3/4 oz.) can condensed golden mushroom soup

1 (4 oz.) can sliced mushrooms

1 (8 oz.) carton sour cream

Cut the steaks into bite-size pieces and brown with the onion in a skillet with a little vegetable oil. When browned, stir in the soup and mushrooms. Simmer until the steaks are tender. Stir in the sour cream, heat through and serve over cooked rice or pasta.

PREP TIME: 15 minutes | COOK TIME: 1 hour | SERVES: 2 to 3

SPICY BAKED BARBECUED RABBIT

1 rabbit

1 cup ketchup

1/4 cup Worcestershire

1 Tablespoon vinegar

3 Tablespoons lemon juice

Salt

1 teaspoon cayenne

Preheat the oven to 350°.

Mix the ketchup, Worcestershire, vinegar, lemon juice, salt and cayenne to make the barbecue sauce. Bake the rabbit in the oven in a pan with a little water for 45 minutes, or until tender. Pour the barbecue sauce over the rabbit and continue baking for another hour, basting often.

PREP TIME: 10 minutes | **COOK TIME:** 1 hour and 45 minutes | **SERVES:** 2 to 4

HUNTING TIP

Match your camo clothing to the time of year and type of foliage where you will be hunting. Choose patterns with more greenery for the early season and patterns with more woody features during the late season.

BAKED RABBIT

1 rabbit, cut into serving pieces

Melted margarine

Finely crushed Ritz® crackers

Preheat the oven to 325°.

Dip the rabbit pieces in melted margarine and roll in the crushed Ritz® crackers. Bake at 300° until tender.

PREP TIME: 15 minutes | **COOK TIME:** 2 1/2 to 3 hours | **SERVES:** 2 to 4

GRILLED BARBECUED RABBIT

2 rabbits

1/4 cup butter

1/4 cup shortening

1/4 cup lemon juice

Barbecue sauce (recipe below)

Parboil the rabbits in water, salt and pepper in a covered pot until the thick parts are tender to the touch of a fork. Remove from the pan and cook over a charcoal fire for 30 to 45 minutes. In a small saucepan on the stovetop, melt the butter and shortening; add the lemon juice. While cooking the rabbits, baste often with the lemon-butter mixture. During the last 15 minutes of grilling, baste the rabbits frequently with the barbecue sauce.

BARBECUE SAUCE

1 medium onion, finely chopped

2 Tablespoons butter

2 Tablespoons vinegar

2 Tablespoons brown sugar

4 Tablespoons lemon juice

1 cup ketchup

3 Tablespoons Worcestershire

1/4 Tablespoon prepared mustard

1/4 cup water

Salt, to taste

Brown the onions and butter in a saucepan. Mix, when browned, with the vinegar, brown sugar, lemon juice, ketchup, Worcestershire, mustard, water and salt. Allow to simmer 30 minutes over low heat.

PREP TIME: 10 minutes | **COOK TIME:** 1 hour | **SERVES:** 4 to 8

DUCK BREAST SALAD

submitted by **CLARK BRENNAN**

3 cups balsamic vinegar
3/4 cup walnut oil (peanut oil can be substituted)
5 teaspoons green peppercorns
1 cup sliced red onion
5 teaspoons chopped garlic
3/4 teaspoon salt
6 (6 to 8 oz.) skinless duck breasts
3 heads romaine lettuce, chopped into bite-size pieces

In a large bowl, combine the balsamic vinegar, walnut oil, green peppercorns, onion, garlic and salt. Place the duck breasts in a single layer in a shallow dish and cover with the vinegar mixture. Marinate in the refrigerator for 2 hours, turning the breasts once.

Preheat a grill or broiler.

Remove the duck from the marinade and grill or broil about 10 minutes until medium rare. Let the breasts cool for 10 minutes, then cut them on the diagonal into thin slices. While the duck is cooling, place the marinade, along with any juices from the duck, in a saucepan and reduce by a third.

Mound a bed of chopped romaine on six plates and fan slices of duck on top of the lettuce. Spoon the reduced marinade over each salad and serve.

PREP TIME: 10 minutes | **MARINATE:** 2 hours | **COOK TIME:** 20 minutes | **SERVES:** 6

INCREASING FISHING ROD SENSITIVITY *by Shaw Grigsby*

One of the crucial aspects of fishing is being able to feel your bait movement, and to feel the strike of a fish. A good way to increase your sensitivity (what you feel) is to move your grip so you have direct contact with the line during the retrieve of the bait. I cradle the reel in the palm of my hand and have the line ride across my index finger. Another way is to move your hand forward of the reel, holding the foregrip of the rod in your lower three fingers, and use your index finger and thumb to hold the line. This allows you to feel directly down the line to the bait, and the strike. Holding the rod gently will also greatly increase sensitivity, every movement of the bait will then be transferred to your hands. Don't hold your rod so loosely that you let a fish steal it. One other tip for sensitivity is to use superbraids. These braided lines have minimal stretch which helps you feel the bait and the strike, plus gives extra hook setting power.

SMOKED MULLET DIP

submitted by SHAW GRIGSBY

2 cups smoked mullet
1/2 cup buttermilk
1/2 cup mayonnaise
1 teaspoon instant (dry) Italian salad dressing mix

Mix above ingredients together in an electric mixer. Be sure to check mullet well and remove small bones before using. Let dip sit in refrigerator for several hours before serving.

This is a great spread on crackers or bread.

PREP TIME: 10 minutes | **CHILL TIME:** 5 hours | **SERVES:** 8 to 10

GERMAN-STYLE RABBIT

1 rabbit

1/4 pound bacon

Salt and pepper

2 Tablespoons butter

2 Tablespoons potato flour

1 pint sour cream

1 teaspoon salt

Dash of pepper

Preheat the oven to 350°.

Singe the rabbit after it has been carefully cleaned, wash it in several cold water rinses and cut it into 5 pieces. Fry the bacon in an ovenproof skillet until the fat is fried out. Add the rabbit to the skillet, cook until brown and then dust with salt and pepper.

Cover the skillet and bake the rabbit in the oven for about 1 hour. Remove the rabbit from the pan and place on a dish. Add the butter to the pan and stir until the butter browns; then add the potato flour. Mix well and add the sour cream. Stir until boiling. Add a teaspoon salt and a dash of pepper; pour the sauce over the rabbit.

PREP TIME: 15 minutes | **COOK TIME:** 1 hour and 30 minutes | **SERVES:** 2 to 4

NOT-SO-SPICY FRIED FISH

submitted by SHAW GRIGSBY

20 oz. Yellow Mustard

3 oz. Tabasco® (or more if you like things spicy)

Cornmeal

Fish - cut into pieces for frying

Mix the Tabasco® and mustard together. Dip dry fish pieces into mustard and Tabasco® mix, then into cornmeal and fry (time will depend on type of fish and size of pieces).

PREP TIME: 10 minutes | COOK TIME: 15 minutes

BEER BATTERED FISH

10 to 12 fish fillets

2 cups all purpose flour

1 egg

1 Tablespoon garlic salt

1 teaspoon salt

1 Tablespoon lemon pepper

1 can beer

1 cup cornflake crumbs or cornmeal

1 Tablespoon vegetable oil

Mix the flour, egg, garlic, salt and lemon pepper in a large bowl. Add the beer until the batter is thin, but not watery. Dip dry fish fillets in the batter, then roll in the cornflakes or cornmeal. Heat vegetable oil in a skillet and fry the fish until golden brown.

PREP TIME: 10 minutes | **COOK TIME:** 15 minutes | **SERVES:** 10 to 12

FISHING SPOTTED SEATROUT

Live shrimp is the bait of choice for most seatrout fishing, however if you are going for a trophy size fish live small fish are a better choice. These are usually fished below a popping cork. Dead bait such as mullet strips, shrimp and pinfish can be fished much the same way as live bait.

MUSTARD FRIED FISH

12 panfish or 6 larger fish fillets

1 (16 oz.) carton sour cream

1 cup prepared mustard

3 cups yellow cornmeal

Salt and pepper

Peanut oil

Coat the fish with the sour cream and mustard and let stand for 20 minutes in the refrigerator. Season the cornmeal with salt and pepper to taste before dredging the fish in the mixture. Deep-fry the fish in hot peanut oil, using either a cast iron skillet or deep fryer.

PREP TIME: 25 minutes | COOK TIME: 10 minutes | SERVES: 4 to 6

HERB FISH

1 pound fish fillets or panfish

1/2 cup all purpose flour

1 egg

1/2 Tablespoon milk

1 (1 pound) box saltine crackers, crushed

1/2 teaspoon parsley flakes

1/2 teaspoon sweet basil

1/4 teaspoon oregano

1/8 teaspoon garlic powder

1/2 cup grated Parmesan cheese

1/2 cup butter-flavored shortening

Pat the fish fillets dry with paper towels. Dredge the fish in the flour and shake off the excess. Beat the egg and milk together in a bowl. In a separate bowl, mix the crackers, parsley, basil, oregano, garlic powder and Parmesan cheese. Dip the fish in the egg mixture, then in the cracker mix. In a frying pan, heat the shortening to 425° to 450°. Place the breaded fish in the pan, skin side up. Fry until golden brown.

PREP TIME: 15 minutes | **COOK TIME:** 15 minutes | **SERVES:** 4

CAJUN FILLETS

1/2 cup all purpose flour or pancake mix

1/4 cup milk

1 egg

1 cup cornmeal

1 Tablespoon Cajun seasoning

1/2 teaspoon salt

1/4 teaspoon pepper

1 pound fish fillets

Vegetable oil

Mix the flour, milk and egg in a small bowl. Mix the cornmeal, Cajun seasoning, salt and pepper in another small bowl. Dip the fillets in the wet mixture to completely moisten the surface; then roll in the dry mixture. Fry the fillets in the oil in a medium-size skillet until both sides are golden brown. Serve with pepper or Tabasco®.

PREP TIME: 15 minutes | **COOK TIME:** 20 minutes | **SERVES:** 4

CREAM CHEESE FISH BAKE

1 (3 oz.) package cream cheese

1 cup uncooked macaroni

1 (10 3/4 oz.) can condensed cream of mushroom soup

1 1/2 cups fish, cooked and flaked

1/4 cup onion, chopped

1/4 cup green pepper, chopped

2 Tablespoons prepared mustard

1/4 teaspoon salt

1/4 cup milk

1/2 cup cornflake crumbs

Preheat the oven to 375°.

Allow the cream cheese to soften at room temperature. Prepare the macaroni according to package directions. Drain. Blend the soup and cream cheese with an electric mixer. Stir in the macaroni, fish, onion, green pepper, mustard, salt and milk. Place the mixture in a 1 1/2 quart dish. Sprinkle with the cornflake crumbs. Bake for 20 to 25 minutes.

PREP TIME: 15 minutes | **COOK TIME:** 35 minutes | **SERVES:** 4

GRILLED BARBECUED CATFISH

6 small to medium catfish

1 teaspoon Worcestershire

1/4 teaspoon paprika

1/2 cup salad oil

1/4 cup white vinegar

1/4 cup ketchup

2 Tablespoons sugar

1/4 teaspoon salt

1/4 teaspoon pepper

Clean and filet the catfish; catfish should be skinned for best results. Combine the Worcestershire, paprika, salad oil, vinegar, ketchup, sugar, salt and pepper. Place the fish in the mixture for 30 minutes before grilling. Cook 3 to 4 inches from hot coals (for a gas grill cook on high heat) on a well-greased grill for about 5 minutes per side, or until the fish tests done. Brush often with the sauce while grilling.

PREP TIME: 40 minutes | **MARINATE:** 30 minutes | **COOK TIME:** 10 minutes | **SERVES:** 3 to 6

CAJUN CATFISH

2 to 3 pounds sliced fish

1 envelope Shake & Bake® for pork

3 Tablespoons flour, sifted

1 cup instant potato flakes

4 Tablespoons cornmeal

Salt and pepper

1/2 cup buttermilk

Hot sauce

Vegetable oil

Mix the Shake & Bake®, flour, potato flakes and cornmeal. Salt and pepper the fish to taste. Mix the buttermilk and hot sauce and pour over the fish. Toss to coat evenly. Press the dry mixture on each piece of fish, coating well. Pan-fry in oil until brown. Turn with a spatula to prevent breaking.

PREP TIME: 10 minutes | **COOK TIME:** 20 minutes | **SERVES:** 4 to 6

SOUTHERN FRIED FISH

12 catfish fillets, halved

Vegetable oil

1/4 cup prepared mustard

1/2 teaspoon paprika

1/2 cup all purpose flour

2 cups yellow cornmeal

Salt and pepper

Cayenne

2 cups buttermilk

1/4 cup Tabasco®

Heat the oil in a large skillet or deep-fat fryer. Combine the mustard, paprika, flour, cornmeal, salt, pepper and cayenne, to taste, in a medium mixing bowl. Add the buttermilk and Tabasco® and mix well. Dip the fish in the buttermilk mixture, dust with the flour, dip again in the mixture and roll in the cornmeal. Drop the fish into the hot oil and cook 6 to 8 minutes, or until brown. Drain well on paper towels before serving.

PREP TIME: 15 minutes | **COOK TIME:** 10 minutes | **SERVES:** 6 to 12

HERB-BAKED CATFISH

1 pound catfish

1 Tablespoon butter

1 cup milk

2 Tablespoons all purpose flour

1/4 teaspoon salt

1/4 teaspoon garlic salt

1/8 teaspoon pepper

1/8 teaspoon dried thyme

Dash of oregano

1/4 cup green onions, sliced

Paprika

Preheat the oven to 350°.

Place the fish in a baking dish. Dot with the butter and set aside. Thoroughly blend the milk and flour in a pan. Cook over medium heat, stirring until the sauce thickens and bubbles. Cook and stir 1 minute longer. Stir in the salt, garlic salt, pepper, thyme, oregano and green onion. Pour the sauce over the fish. Sprinkle with paprika. Bake in the oven, uncovered, for 20 to 25 minutes.

PREP TIME: 20 minutes | **COOK TIME:** 35 minutes | **SERVES:** 4

BLACKENED CATFISH

6 catfish fillets

2 teaspoons paprika

2 1/2 teaspoons salt

1 teaspoon onion powder

1 1/2 teaspoons garlic

1 1/2 teaspoons cayenne

2 teaspoons lemon pepper marinade

1 teaspoon ground thyme

1 1/2 teaspoons basil

8 oz. (1 stick) unsalted butter, melted

Lemon wedges

Heat a skillet over high heat until a drop of water sizzles in the pan, or about 10 minutes. Combine the paprika, salt, onion powder, garlic, cayenne, lemon pepper marinade, thyme and basil in a medium bowl. Keep fillets cold until ready to use. Dip each fillet in the melted butter, sprinkle the seasoning mix on both sides and place them on waxed paper while preparing other fillets. Place 3 fillets in the hot skillet and drizzle each piece of fish with 1 Tablespoon of melted butter. (There will be a lot of smoke. Make sure you are in a well-ventilated place.) Cook quickly, about 2 minutes per side. Remove and repeat the process until all fillets are cooked. Serve immediately with the lemon wedges.

PREP TIME: 15 minutes | **COOK TIME:** 12 minutes | **SERVES:** 6

FISHING CATFISH

Find areas where moving water makes a sharp bend in the channel to maximize catfishing success during the hot summertime. Catfish are looking for an easy meal when the water warms and their metabolism decreases. Current breaks like this will be where they wait to ambush food as it slowly drifts down current.

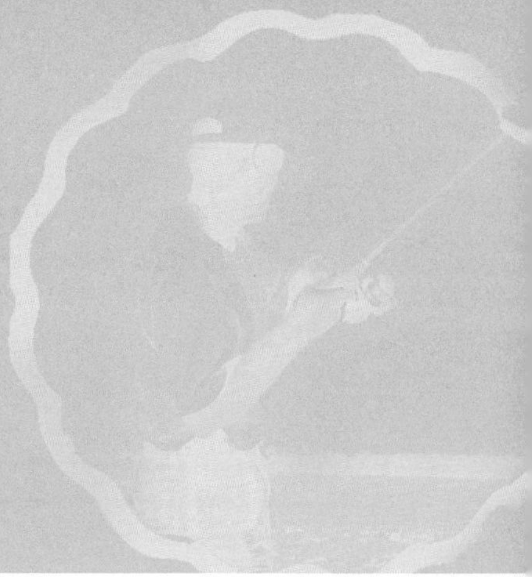

YANKEE CATFISH STEW

5 pounds catfish

1/2 pound bacon, diced

3 pounds red potatoes, diced

2 pounds white onions, diced

5 cups water

6 hard-cooked eggs, diced

1 (4 oz.) can pimiento, drained and diced

1 (6 oz.) can evaporated milk

Salt and pepper

Fry the fish (use a batter with cornmeal, milk and seasonings) until it flakes when poked with a fork. Fry the bacon until crisp and remove from the skillet. Fry the potatoes and onion in the bacon drippings until tender. Place the fish in 4 cups of the water in a Dutch oven. Add the bacon, potatoes, onion, eggs and pimiento. Simmer for 1 to 1 1/2 hours, adding remaining water if needed. Add the milk, stirring constantly, while seasoning with the salt and pepper to taste.

PREP TIME: 15 minutes | **COOK TIME:** 2 1/2 hours | **SERVES:** 10 to 15

GRILLED PARMESAN CRAPPIE

Fresh crappie fillets
4 Tablespoons lemon juice
Butter or margarine
Seasoned salt
Fresh grated Parmesan cheese
1 medium green pepper, diced
1 medium onion, diced

Fold a sheet of aluminum foil in two and form into a small "dish." Pour enough lemon juice in the foil to cover the bottom and put the fillets in the juice. Place a generous amount of butter on top of each fillet and sprinkle each with seasoned salt and Parmesan cheese. Add the diced green peppers and onions and use another piece of foil to completely enclose the fillets by folding over all edges. Grill for 5 to 6 minutes on each side. Drain juices and serve.

PREP TIME: 15 minutes | **COOK TIME:** 12 to 15 minutes | **SERVES:** 6

OVEN-FRIED CRAPPIE

1 pound crappie fillets

1/3 cup cornmeal

1/3 cup bread crumbs

1/2 teaspoon paprika

1/4 teaspoon dill weed

Salt and pepper

1/3 cup milk

3 Tablespoons melted butter or margarine

Preheat the oven to 425°.

Cut the fillets into desired serving sizes. Combine the cornmeal, bread crumbs, paprika and dill weed in a medium bowl. Add salt and pepper to taste. Pour the milk into a small bowl. Dip the fish in the milk and roll in the dry mixture. Place the fillets on a cookie sheet or baking pan and drizzle butter over each fillet. Bake at 425° for about 12 minutes, or until the fillets are moist and flaky.

PREP TIME: 15 minutes | **COOK TIME:** 20 minutes | **SERVES:** 4 to 6

BAKED PARMESAN CRAPPIE

1 to 2 pounds crappie fillets

1/4 cup Parmesan cheese

1/4 cup seasoned bread crumbs

1 Tablespoon melted butter or margarine

4 Tablespoons fresh parsley

Preheat the oven to 325°.

Mix the Parmesan cheese, bread crumbs, butter and parsley in a small bowl. Place fillets in a greased baking pan and sprinkle seasoning mixture over them. Bake at 325° for 15 to 20 minutes.

PREP TIME: 10 minutes | COOK TIME: 15 to 20 minutes | SERVES: 4

FISHING CRAPPIE

When crappie roam open water and they are hard to find, drift or slow troll jigs with an electric motor. Many dedicated crappie fisherman drift or troll with so many rods sticking out over the sides of their boats that the method has become known as "spider fishing."

POTATO CRAPPIE FILLETS

1 pound crappie fillets

1/3 cup all purpose flour

Salt and pepper

Blackened seasoning (optional)

2 eggs

1 cup instant potato flakes

Vegetable oil

Combine the flour, salt and pepper to taste in a medium bowl (if using the blackened seasoning add it, too). Beat the eggs in a small bowl until smooth. Pour the potato flakes onto a large plate or wax paper on the countertop. Roll the fillets in the seasoning mixture, dip in the eggs to wet, and then roll in the potato flakes. Fry in the oil in a heavy, medium sized skillet until golden brown.

PREP TIME: 10 minutes | **COOK TIME:** 20 minutes | **SERVES:** 4

GRILLED SNAPPER

6 to 8 whole snapper

1 stick butter or margarine

1 cup green onion, chopped

Salt and pepper

Garlic powder

2 Tablespoons dehydrated parsley flakes

Inside each snapper cavity place 1 Tablespoon of the butter, some chopped onion, salt, pepper and garlic powder to taste. Sprinkle the outside with parsley flakes and a little salt and pepper. Double wrap the snapper, one to a package, in aluminum foil. Place on the grill, cook 7 to 10 minutes on one side, turn, and cook 5 minutes more.

PREP TIME: 10 minutes | **COOK TIME:** 10 minutes | **SERVES:** 6 to 8

BROILED TROUT

2 pounds trout fillets

2 Tablespoons melted butter

Topping (recipe follows)

Parmesan cheese

Preheat the oven to broil.

Melt the butter in a shallow oven safe pan, add the trout fillets. Place in oven and broil until they flake, turning once. While this is cooking, prepare the topping. When the fillets are done, spoon the topping over them. Sprinkle generously with Parmesan cheese. Serve immediately.

BROILED TROUT TOPPING

1/2 cup fresh mushrooms, sliced

1/4 cup fresh green onions, chopped (include tops)

1 teaspoon butter

Sauté the mushrooms and onions in the butter until slightly tender.

PREP TIME: 5 minutes | COOK TIME: 10 minutes | SERVES: 4

TROUT KABOBS

1 large green pepper

1 quart water

4 small onions (about 1/2 pound)

2 pounds trout or other oily fish fillets or steaks, skin removed

16 French bread cubes, 1 1/2 x 1 1/2" thick

4 metal skewers, 15" long

1 cup margarine or butter

1/4 teaspoon garlic salt

4 lemon wedges

Set the oven to broil or 550°.

Core and seed the pepper, and cut in half. In a 3-quart saucepan, heat the water to boiling. Add the green pepper and onions and cover. Cook over high heat for 4 minutes. Drain. Rinse under cold, running water and drain. Cut the onions in half and cut the green pepper into 1" pieces. Cut the fish into 1" chunks. Alternately thread 2 onion halves, 1/4 of the green pepper pieces, 1/4 of the fish, and 4 bread cubes on each skewer. Place the kabobs on a lightly greased broiler pan. In a 1 quart saucepan, heat the margarine and garlic salt over medium heat until the margarine is melted. Brush the margarine on the fish, bread and vegetables. Broil the kabobs 8 to 9 inches from the heat, turning and brushing with margarine 4 times or until the fish flakes easily at the thickest part, about 8 minutes. Serve the kabobs with the lemon wedges.

PREP TIME: 20 minutes | **COOK TIME:** 12 to 15 minutes | **SERVES:** 4 to 6

BAKED TROUT

4 trout, with or without heads

Fresh lemon juice

Salt and pepper

Lemon slices

Butter

Onion slices (optional)

Parsley flakes

Fresh parsley

Preheat the oven to 325°.

Sprinkle the lemon juice over thoroughly cleaned fish. Salt and pepper the fish to taste; place the lemon slices and pats of the butter on the fish. Raw onion slices may be used, too. Place fish in a baking dish, sprinkle the fish with parsley flakes. Bake 1 to 1 1/2 pounds fish for 30 to 40 minutes; fish 2 1/2 pounds or heavier take 1 to 1 1/4 hours. Serve with additional lemon slices and fresh parsley.

PREP TIME: 10 minutes | **COOK TIME:** 40 minutes to 1 1/2 hours | **SERVES:** 2 to 4

SASSY RAINBOW TROUT

4 rainbow trout fillets

Salt and pepper

4 Tablespoons olive oil

2 egg yolks

2 sticks butter or margarine

1 Tablespoon lemon juice

1 cup cooked chopped shrimp

1/2 cup crabmeat

1/2 cup sliced mushrooms

2 Tablespoons dry white wine

2 to 4 drops Tabasco®

Preheat the oven to 375°.

Dry the fillets and season with salt and pepper to taste. Place in a baking dish, add the oil, and bake in the oven for about 20 minutes. Make the sauce while the fish bake. Put the 2 egg yolks in the top of a double boiler over hot, but not boiling, water and beat until slightly thickened. Melt the butter and slowly add it to the egg yolks, stirring constantly until the mixture thickens. Add the lemon juice, shrimp, crabmeat, mushrooms, wine and Tabasco®. Mix well and season to taste with salt and pepper. Stir and cook for 10 minutes longer. Raise the oven temperature to broil. Place the baked fillets on an ovenproof platter. Spoon the sauce over the fish and place it under the broiler, until slightly browned.

PREP TIME: 20 minutes | **COOK TIME:** 30 minutes | **SERVES:** 2 to 4

BAKED TROUT WITH TOMATO AND ONION

1 pound trout

1 Tablespoon parsley, chopped

1 Tablespoon lemon juice

3/4 teaspoon salt

3 Tablespoons olive oil

1 medium onion, thinly sliced

1 clove garlic, minced

1 large tomato, thinly sliced

1 lemon, thinly sliced

2 Tablespoons white wine (or water)

Preheat the oven to 350°.

Arrange the fish in an 8" or 9" square baking dish. Sprinkle with the parsley, lemon juice and salt. Heat the oil in a skillet and sauté the onion and garlic until limp. Top the fish with the onion mixture and oil from skillet. Arrange the tomato slices on top of the onion mixture and place the lemon slices on top. Pour wine (or water) over all and bake in the oven for 30 to 35 minutes, or until fish flakes easily.

PREP TIME: 15 minutes | COOK TIME: 40 to 45 minutes | SERVES: 4

FISHING TIP *by Clark Brennan*

Red snapper are a structure oriented fish with wrecks, submerged reefs and petroleum rigs among the man-made and natural habitats they prefer. Snappers feed on most any animal they can find and are not particularly selective. Cigar minnows and poggies are good choices for baits, but since snapper tend to be nibblers and browsers rather than strikers, a soft touch is required to be productive.

TROUT NANCY

submitted by CLARK BRENNAN

8 trout fillets (drum or redfish can be substituted)
Salt and pepper
All purpose flour
1/2 stick butter
1 1/2 pounds lump crabmeat, picked over to remove any shell or cartilage (blanched crawfish tails may be substituted)
1/2 cup capers
1 1/2 cups lemon butter sauce

Season the trout fillets on both sides with salt and pepper and then dredge in flour. Melt the butter in a large sauté pan and cook the fish over medium heat until flaky, about 4 minutes per side. Remove the fish from the pan and place in a warm oven until serving.

Cook the crabmeat and capers briefly in the pan drippings until hot.

Place trout fillets on plates and top with the crabmeat and capers. Spoon lemon butter sauce over the fish and serve.

PREP TIME: 10 minutes | **COOK TIME:** 10 minutes | **SERVES:** 4 to 8

SMOKED TROUT

6 trout fillets

1 stick butter

1 cup honey

3 teaspoons lemon pepper

1 teaspoon blackened seasoning

Put hickory sawdust in the bottom of a stove-top smoker and heat to medium.

Mix the butter, honey, lemon pepper and blackened seasoning. Cut grooves into the fillet and brush the fillet well with the marinade, filling the grooves. Put trout fillets on a rack in the smoker, cover with a lid, and cook for 15 to 20 minutes. Slide the lid open and marinate the meat again. Close the lid and cook for another 5 to 10 minutes.

Note: An outdoor smoker also works well for this dish.

PREP TIME: 10 minutes | COOK TIME: 20 to 30 minutes | SERVES: 6

BROILED STRIPER FILLETS

2 pounds fresh striper or hybrid fillets

1/3 cup orange juice

1 Tablespoon soy sauce

1 teaspoon salt

Dash of pepper

1/2 stick butter or margarine, melted

Preheat the oven to broil.

Cut the fillets into serving-size portions. Mix the orange juice, soy sauce, salt, pepper and butter. Place the fish in a greased broiler pan and brush the fillets with the sauce. Broil 3" from the heat for 4 to 5 minutes with occasional basting. Turn carefully and brush with sauce. Broil for another 4 to 5 minutes with occasional basting. The fish is done when flaky.

PREP TIME: 5 minutes | **COOK TIME:** 10 minutes | **SERVES:** 3 to 6

SAUTÉED STRIPE

4 stripe fillets

1 bell pepper, sliced

1 medium onion, sliced

Garlic cloves

Olive oil

Lea & Perrins® White Wine Worcestershire

Salt and pepper

Paprika

Lemon or lime juice

Melted butter

Place sliced bell pepper, onion and a few cloves of garlic into an aluminum pan big enough to fit on a grill. Put enough olive oil in the pan to just cover the bottom and set it on the rack of a hot grill. Add the peppers, onions and garlic. Sauté the vegetables for a few minutes in the oil. Add the stripe fillets and continue to sauté, adding several dashes of white wine Worcestershire (not too much or it will overpower the flavor). Add the pepper, salt, paprika and lemon or lime juice and some melted butter. Cook the fish for 10 minutes or so, or until it flakes with a fork.

PREP TIME: 15 minutes | **COOK TIME:** 20 minutes | **SERVES:** 4

ZESTY BASS

4 (5- to 8-oz.) bass fillets with skin

1 cup onion, finely chopped

1 cup parsley, chopped

2 Tablespoons olive or peanut oil

1 Tablespoon garlic, finely chopped

4 cups tomatoes, peeled and chopped

Ground red pepper

2 cups Burgundy wine

1 Tablespoon soy sauce

Salt and pepper

Place the onions and parsley in the oil and sauté 3 to 5 minutes. Add the garlic, tomatoes, red pepper, wine and soy sauce. Cook until the onions are translucent, about 10 minutes. Lightly season the fillets with salt and pepper to taste. Place them, skin side up, on a medium-hot grill for 3 minutes. Turn and cook 2 minutes more. Place on aluminum foil in a grill-safe pan on the grill; top with sauce. Close the top of the grill and cook 10 minutes.

PREP TIME: 20 minutes | **COOK TIME:** 25 minutes | **SERVES:** 4

ORANGE BASS

4 bass fillets

Orange juice

Garlic salt

All purpose flour

Vegetable oil

Soak the fillets in the refrigerator in a mixture of orange juice and garlic salt overnight, or for at least 6 hours. Turn the fillets once during soaking. Drain the juice from the fillets. Coat the fillets with the flour and fry in oil.

PREP TIME: 5 minutes | **MARINATE:** 6 hours or overnight | **COOK TIME:** 15 minutes | **SERVES:** 4

POTATO CRUSTED WALLEYE

1 1/2 pounds sauger/walleye fillets
1/2 cup all purpose flour
1 teaspoon paprika
1/2 teaspoon salt
1/4 teaspoon pepper
Garlic powder
Parsley
1 cup instant potato flakes
2 eggs, beaten
Vegetable oil
Lemon wedges
Tartar sauce

Combine the flour, paprika, salt, pepper, garlic powder and parsley in a shallow bowl. Put the potato flakes on a plate. Dredge the fillets in the flour mixture, dip them in the eggs, and roll them in the potato flakes. Heat about 1/2" of oil in a large skillet. Fry the fillets 2 to 3 minutes per side, until golden brown, and drain on a paper-towel-covered plate. Serve with lemon wedges and tartar sauce.

PREP TIME: 15 minutes | **COOK TIME:** 10 minutes | **SERVES:** 4 to 5

FISHING TIP *by Shaw Grigsby*

Be meticulous about the little details when you are preparing for a fishing trip. Make sure you and your equipment are ready. Check to see if your reels are working properly. Check the drag and make sure it is set for the correct pound test line and types fish. The guides should be secure and free of nicks, especially at the tip. Your hooks should be dangerously sharp, especially those on crankbaits. Check the line on your reels to see if it is old or has rough spots; if so, change it. Be sure to retie after every decent fish or after several small ones. If your line is breaking at the knot, consider changing your knot to one such as the polymar. You never know when the fish of a lifetime might strike, so be prepared.

LEMON FRIED BLUEGILL

1 1/2 pounds bluegill

1 cup all purpose flour, plus additional flour for dredging

2 teaspoons lemon peel, grated

1/2 teaspoon salt

1/4 teaspoon pepper

1 cup water

Vegetable oil

Blend 1 cup flour, lemon peel, salt and pepper. Add the water, mix and chill for 30 minutes. Heat 2" of oil in a fryer to 375°. Coat the fish with additional flour and dip in the batter. Fry for about 3 minutes. Drain on paper towels.

PREP TIME: 40 minutes | COOK TIME: 15 minutes | SERVES: 4

ORANGE WALLEYE

4 walleye

Butter or margarine

1 orange, quartered

Sesame seeds

Garlic powder

Onion powder

Parsley

Parmesan cheese (optional)

Preheat the oven to 425°.

Rub the bottom of a glass baking dish with a small amount of butter or margarine. Lay the fillets in one layer in the dish. Squeeze 2 or 3 orange quarters over the fish; then sprinkle the sesame seeds, garlic powder, onion powder and parsley over the top. Sprinkle a little Parmesan cheese over the top if desired. Bake for 10 to 15 minutes, or until the fish flakes easily with a fork.

PREP TIME: 10 minutes | **COOK TIME:** 15 minutes | **SERVES:** 4

WALLEYE WITH RICE STUFFING

2 to 2 1/2 pounds walleye

1 (6 oz.) package wild and long grain rice mix

1 teaspoon instant chicken bouillon granules

1/2 cup fresh mushrooms, sliced (optional)

1/2 cup celery, chopped

2 Tablespoons butter

1 (2 oz.) jar pimientos, drained and sliced

1/8 teaspoon ground sage

Preheat the oven to 375°.

Prepare the rice as directed on the package, adding the bouillon granules to the water. Grease a broiler pan or 13 x 9" baking pan. In a small skillet, cook and stir the mushrooms and celery in the butter over medium heat until the mushrooms are tender, about 5 minutes. Stir in the pimiento and sage. Stir the vegetables into the rice. Place the fish on the broiler or baking pan. Stuff with the rice mixture, placing any extra stuffing around the fish. Cover only the rice with foil. Bake until the fish flakes easily at the backbone, 20 to 25 minutes.

PREP TIME: 20 minutes | **COOK TIME:** 30 to 35 minutes | **SERVES:** 4 to 6

BASS–STUFFED MUSHROOM CAPS

1 (8 oz.) bass fillet

6 Tablespoons sour cream

1 teaspoon curry powder

1/2 teaspoon salt

Pinch of cayenne

1 rib celery, diced

4 green onions, diced

16 (2” diameter) mushrooms

2 Tablespoons butter, melted

Cook the bass fillet in the microwave. Chill for 30 to 60 minutes and then flake. Stir together the sour cream, curry powder, salt and cayenne. Fold in the diced celery, onions and flaked fish. Cover and refrigerate for at least one hour.

Preheat the oven to 375°.

Remove the mushroom stems. Rinse the caps and dry. Set on a lightly oiled baking sheet. Brush the mushrooms with the melted butter, then add a dollop of the bass mixture. Bake for 15 minutes.

PREP TIME: 20 minutes | **CHILL:** 2 hours | **COOK TIME:** 15 minutes | **SERVES:** 2 to 4

FISHING TIP *by Earl Bentz*

Live shrimp is the bait of choice for most trout fishing; however, if you are going for a trophy size fish, live small fish are a better choice. These are usually fished below a popping cork. Dead bait such as mullet strips, shrimp and pinfish can be fished much the same way as live bait.

MALLARD SALAD

submitted by EARL BENTZ

3 ducks
2 hard-boiled eggs, chopped
3 Tablespoons sweet pickle relish
2 Tablespoons mayonnaise
1 large onion, chopped
Celery, chopped (equal the amount of onion)
Pepper

In roasting pan, roast ducks until tender. Let cool and pull meat off. Finely chop meat in food processor. Add remaining ingredients. MOST IMPORTANT LAST STEP: From the Tablespoon opening on a can of fresh black pepper, completely cover the top of the salad with pepper, then stir. Repeat this step once more before serving.

PREP TIME: 20 minutes | COOK TIME: 1 hour | SERVES: 4

COGNAC QUAIL

4 to 6 quail

8 shallots, chopped

4 Tablespoons butter

1/2 cup Cognac

2 cups chicken broth

Salt and pepper

1 cup whipping cream

Preheat the oven to 350°.

In a heavy skillet on the stovetop, brown the quail with the shallots in butter. Pour the cognac over the quail and stir lightly over low heat, until the Cognac evaporates. Place the quail and the shallots in an oven safe dish and cover with the chicken broth. Season with salt and pepper. Cook in the oven 30 minutes. Pour the whipping cream over the quail and serve with wild rice, using the gravy from the oven dish.

PREP TIME: 15 minutes | **COOK TIME:** 50 minutes | **SERVES:** 4 to 6

QUAIL OR GROUSE SUPREME

3 quail or 1 grouse

1/2 teaspoon poultry seasoning

2 Tablespoons onion, chopped

1 Tablespoon green pepper, chopped

1/4 cup mushrooms, chopped

Salt and pepper

1/2 teaspoon sage

2 slices bacon

Soak the quail or grouse in salted water for 1 hour in the refrigerator. Dry thoroughly.

Preheat the oven to 375°.

Combine the poultry seasoning, onion, green pepper, mushrooms, salt, pepper and sage. Stuff the birds with the mixture and truss with poultry skewers. Wrap the birds with bacon. Place any leftover stuffing on the birds, cover and roast in the oven for 1 hour or until browned.

PREP TIME: 1 hour and 20 minutes | COOK TIME: 1 hour | SERVES: 3

QUAIL AND MUSHROOMS

6 quail

6 slices bacon

Salt and pepper

1/2 pound mushroom caps

1 bunch green onions

3 Tablespoons melted butter

2 Tablespoons prepared mustard

1/4 teaspoon dry ginger

1 cup orange marmalade

Preheat the oven to 325°.

Wrap the bacon around the birds and arrange in rows on a large sheet of heavy-duty aluminum foil. Season with salt and pepper to taste. Sauté the mushrooms and green onions in the butter; pour over the quail. Seal with a double wrap of foil and bake for 1 hour. Combine the mustard, ginger and marmalade and pour over quail to serve.

PREP TIME: 10 minutes | **COOK TIME:** 1 hour 15 minutes | **SERVES:** 6

SMOTHERED DOVES

6 doves

1 stick butter

2 Tablespoons all purpose flour

2 cups water

Salt and pepper

1 Tablespoon Worcestershire

2 Tablespoons lemon juice

Preheat the oven to 350°.

Melt the butter in a skillet. Add the flour and cook until smooth and brown. Add water gradually, stirring until thickened. Stir in salt, pepper, Worcestershire and lemon juice. Arrange the doves in a baking dish; pour the sauce over the doves and cover the dish. Bake for 2 hours. Baste occasionally; add water if necessary.

PREP TIME: 5 minutes | **COOK TIME:** 2 hours | **SERVES:** 4 to 6

FLAMING ROAST DOVES

12 doves

Salt and pepper

24 juniper berries

1 stick butter

1/4 cup Cognac

Preheat the oven to 350°.

Salt and pepper the doves to taste; place 2 juniper berries inside each. In a heavy, ovenproof skillet brown the birds with the butter. Cover the skillet and bake for 30 minutes. Remove from the oven and uncover. In a ladle, warm the Cognac, ignite it, and pour over the birds.

PREP TIME: 10 minutes | **COOK TIME:** 45 minutes | **SERVES:** 6 to 8

TIPSY DOVES

18 dove breasts, or breasts with legs

1 teaspoon salt

1 bay leaf

2 (10 3/4 oz.) cans condensed cream of mushroom or cream of chicken soup

1 cup water

1 cup onion, chopped

1 Tablespoon dried parsley

1 teaspoon celery seeds

1 cup fresh mushrooms, sliced

1 cup white wine

Place the dove breasts in a large skillet and barely cover with water. Add salt to taste and the bay leaf. Simmer for 20 minutes, turning once. Drain; discard the bay leaf. Combine the soup and 1 cup water in a large bowl and stir to mix. Add the onion, parsley and celery seeds. Mix well and pour over the doves. Heat to simmer, cover, and continue to simmer for 30 minutes. Add fresh mushrooms, stir and simmer an additional 10 minutes. Add the wine, stirring to mix. Heat to simmer and serve at once. For best results, use fresh mushrooms and do not overcook them after adding the wine.

PREP TIME: 10 minutes | **COOK TIME:** 1 hour | **SERVES:** 8 to 10

MIKE'S DUCK GUMBO

submitted by MIKE McLEMORE

2 ducks (or 3 to 4 duck breasts)
2 bay leaves
2 cloves garlic, minced
4 or 5 ribs celery, chopped
1 1/2 (12 oz.) packages frozen onions, chopped
or 2 large onions, chopped
1 bell pepper, chopped
1 (1 1/4 pound) package frozen okra
1 (3/4 oz.) package brown gravy mix
3 Tablespoons oil
1 (1 pound) can whole tomatoes
1 teaspoon cracked black pepper
3 Tablespoons parsley flakes
1/2 to 1 teaspoon Tabasco®
1 Tablespoon Worcestershire
Juice of 1/2 lemon
Salt to taste
Cooked rice

Boil ducks and bay leaves in water to cover. Remove ducks when tender; pull meat from bones and chop. Add garlic, celery, onion, bell pepper and okra to broth. In another pan, make roux of gravy mix and oil. Add tomatoes and pepper to roux, then mix with broth. Add parsley and duck. Simmer 2 1/2 to 3 hours, stirring often. Add Tabasco®, Worcestershire, lemon juice, salt and stir well. Serve over rice.

Note: Ham hock, shrimp, or oysters may be added for variety.

PREP TIME: 20 minutes | COOK TIME: 1 1/2 hours | SERVES: 2

PHEASANT RICE BAKE

1 pheasant, cut in pieces

Vinegar or lemon juice

1 package onion soup mix

1 cup rice, cooked or uncooked

1 (10 3/4 oz.) can condensed cream of mushroom soup

1 soup can of milk

1 (8 oz.) can French fried onion rings

Preheat the oven to 350°.

Simmer the pheasant in water with a small amount of the vinegar or lemon juice to help tenderize the bird. Sprinkle the dry soup mix into a buttered casserole dish. Sprinkle the rice over the soup mix. Add the cooked pheasant pieces. Mix the soup and milk, and pour the mixture over the pheasant. Cover and bake in the oven for 1 1/4 hours. Uncover and sprinkle with the onion rings. Cook 15 minutes longer.

PREP TIME: 10 minutes | COOK TIME: 2 hours | SERVES: 4 to 6

PHEASANT WITH WILD RICE

2 pheasants (may be cut in halves)

3 cups water

Salt

3 to 4 Tablespoons cornstarch

1/2 (10 3/4 oz.) can condensed cream of mushroom soup

1/2 (10 3/4 oz.) can condensed cream of celery soup

1/2 (10 3/4 oz.) can condensed cream of chicken soup

1 (8 oz.) box wild rice

Soak the pheasant in water for at least 3 hours in the refrigerator before cooking. Put the birds in a large pot, add the water and salt to taste, and heat to a hard boil. Skim the surface if needed. Reduce the heat and cook slowly until tender. Remove the birds and cool. Strain the broth to remove any bone fragments. Return the broth to the pot and add the cornstarch dissolved in cold water. Add the mushroom, celery and chicken soups to the broth. Remove the meat from the bones and add it to the broth. Simmer for 30 minutes. Cook the rice as directed on the box; serve the pheasant with, or on, a bed of rice.

MARINATE: 3 hours | PREP TIME: 15 minutes | COOK TIME: 1 hour | SERVES: 4 to 6

PHEASANT PASTA

1 cup sour cream

1 cup heavy cream

1 pheasant breast, diced into 1/2" cubes

2 Tablespoons butter

1 cup diced ham

2 (6 oz.) cans tomato paste

1/2 teaspoon lemon-pepper seasoning

1 teaspoon Italian seasoning

1/2 teaspoon pepper

1/4 teaspoon salt

Pinch of dry, crushed red pepper flakes

1 pound pasta

Mix the sour cream and heavy cream in a small bowl and refrigerate for 4 to 6 hours. Brown the breast cubes in a skillet with the melted butter over medium heat. Add the diced ham and cook about 5 minutes. Stir in the tomato paste, lemon-pepper seasoning, Italian seasoning, pepper, salt and red pepper flakes. Lower the heat and simmer 10 minutes. Add the sour cream mixture and cook until heated, stirring constantly. Cook the pasta according to package directions. Serve the sauce over the cooked pasta.

PREP TIME: 4 to 6 hours | **COOK TIME:** 30 minutes | **SERVES:** 3 to 4

GRILLED DUCK

2 duck breasts

1 cup Italian dressing (oil and vinegar style)

Salt and pepper

6 slices bacon

1 tomato, sliced

1 onion, sliced

Remove all the skin and fat from the breasts. Marinate them in a saucepan in the refrigerator with the Italian dressing for approximately 30 minutes. Remove the breasts from the saucepan and add salt and pepper to taste. Wrap the breasts with the bacon. Place the breasts on a foil-lined cookie sheet and cover with the sliced tomatoes and onions. Heat the grill to a medium-high temperature. Allow to cook in a covered grill until three-quarters done. Remove the breasts from the cookie sheet, and place on the grill for braising. Reduce the heat to low and cook until the bacon is done.

PREP TIME: 10 minutes | **MARINATE:** 30 minutes | **COOK TIME:** 45 minutes | **SERVES:** 2 to 4

CONDUCTING BUSINESS IN THE FIELD *by Kelly Powers*

I hunt with the same group of guys everyday and we take our approaches very seriously regarding the manner by which we "conduct business" in the field. There is always one "pit boss," which eliminates second guesses concerning who exactly will call the shots during the hunt. This person will unquestionably lead the way in calling, meaning that he watches every movement made by the birds as they approach or circle the decoy spread. Consequently, only one person is continually looking at the birds rather than four or five pairs of eyes. Through actual experience in hunting with the same core of individuals, I can close my eyes and literally describe where the birds are and what they're doing by just listening to the calling sequence of our crew. The more experience you gain hunting with the same crew day-in and day-out will dramatically increase your success ratio.

SIMPLE DUCK ROAST

1 duck

2 apples, peeled and diced

1 large onion, chopped

Salt and pepper

2/3 cup port

1 teaspoon cornstarch

Lemon juice

Preheat the oven to 450° to 500°.

Clean the cavity of the duck and stuff it with the apples and chopped onion. Season with salt and pepper to taste. Place on a rack (to render the juices and fat) and roast in the oven for about 20 minutes. Remove the bird and keep warm. Drain the fat from the pan; then add to the pan a mixture of the port and cornstarch. Stir to blend and thicken, season with salt and pepper and a squirt of lemon juice and then strain into a sauce boat. Serve the duck with wild rice.

PREP TIME: 20 minutes | **COOK TIME:** 40 minutes | **SERVES:** 2 or 3

DUCK CALLING *by Steve McCadams*

The duck call is practically a musical instrument, requiring time and patience. It's a challenge, but with practice you can master the sounds needed to lure ducks into gunning range.

There are three basic calls used by veteran guides. I use the "hail call" to attract the attention of distant or highflying ducks. Then there's the "feeding call," which is used when the birds are close to keep them at ease. And, in my opinion, the most important of all is the "lonesome hen," which I use to both get their attention and keep their interest.

I'd recommend spending some time with a veteran caller and listening to his sound and sequences of calls. You'll benefit from his experience. And, listening to real ducks is imperative. Find a refuge, swamp or lake where ducks congregate in large numbers and observe their sounds and behavior.

Controlling your airflow is an active ingredient in the recipe for successful calling. Knowing when to breathe and disperse air as you manipulate your tongue and mouth helps emit the various tones.

Try saying the word "tweet" as you begin the high notes of the "hail call." The first three or four bursts of air need to sing the note slightly before tapering off with a series of shorter ones.

For the "feed call" or "chuckle" try uttering the word "tuga" over and over. And, for the "lonesome hen" try saying "ain't" five times, but begin on a higher note and taper off as you run out of air.

Cupping one hand over the call and opening it up as you release the note will help alter your sound, too.

Try recording your technique and play it back to critique yourself.

Adjusting the reed to your satisfaction is a trial and error effort. Minor adjustments can have major influences on the tone.

Don't be afraid to experiment with different calls as wood and acrylic may blow differently. Most reeds are plastic, but a few calls offer metal varieties.

Once you learn to make the basic sounds you'll soon graduate into calling techniques and learn to vary your style and volume. Knowing what call to use, and when, is a timing thing learned only from many mornings in the marsh.

GOLDEN BROWN CRAPPIE FILLETS

submitted by STEVE McCADAMS

10-12 crappie fillets
Milk
Flour
1 Tablespoon Lawry's® Seasoned Salt
Vegetable oil

Soak the fillets overnight in the refrgerator in milk. Then, roll fillets in mixture of flour and 1 Tablespoon of seasoned salt. Fry in vegetable oil until golden brown.

These are great with white northern beans, slaw, French fries and hush puppies.

PREP TIME: 10 minutes | MARINATE: overnight | COOK TIME: 4 minutes | SERVES: 3 to 4

ROASTED DUCK BREAST

4 duck breast fillets

8 slices bacon

1 teaspoon salt

Black pepper

Red pepper

Cinnamon

1 1/2 sticks butter, sliced

1 bay leaf, crushed

1 Tablespoon poultry seasoning

1 teaspoon parsley flakes

Preheat the oven to 350°.

Rinse the fillets, pat dry and wrap in bacon. Sprinkle each breast with salt, black pepper, red pepper and cinnamon. Arrange in a baking dish lined with a large piece of foil. Add the butter slices, sprinkle with the bay leaf and poultry seasoning. Seal the foil tightly and bake 1 1/4 hours.

PREP TIME: 10 minutes | COOK TIME: 1 1/4 hours | SERVES: 4

WADING TIP *by Mike McLemore*

Always carry a couple of large plastic garbage bags in your waterfowl bag along with extra socks and pants. This is in case you fall or step in over your waders. If this horrid event should happen, just pull off your waders, dump out the water, change into the dry pants and socks. Put your feet into the dry garbage bags, one for each leg. Then you can put your waders back on and enjoy the hunt.

BAGGED DUCK

2 to 4 ducks

Turkey-size oven bag

1 (8 oz.) can crushed pineapple

1 (6 oz.) can frozen orange juice

Preheat the oven to 350°.

Place the ducks in the oven bag and into a cooking pan. Pour the crushed pineapple and frozen orange juice over the ducks. Close the bag with its tie and cut 4 to 6 small holes in the bag. Cook for 3 to 4 hours.

Note: You can cook a goose the same way, but cook for 4 1/2 to 5 hours. You may want to quarter the goose.

PREP TIME: 10 minutes | **COOK TIME:** 3 to 4 hours | **SERVES:** 2 to 6

HEARTY DUCK AND BEAN CASSEROLE

4 duck breasts

1 pound dried Great Northern beans

2 quarts water

1/4 teaspoon ground cloves

2 bay leaves

1 large onion, chopped

1 pound mild or hot sausage

1 cup apple juice

1 (6 oz.) can tomato paste

1 teaspoon thyme

1 Tablespoon parsley flakes

Put the beans in water, cover and soak overnight.

Preheat the oven to 375°.

Drain beans and combine with two quarts fresh water in a large saucepan. Add the rinsed duck breasts, cloves and bay leaves to the beans. Bring to a boil, skim the foam and simmer for one hour. Remove and slice the duck breasts. Cook the beans 15 minutes longer. Remove the bay leaves. Drain the beans, reserving the liquid. Cook the onion and sausage until crumbly; drain and add the apple juice, tomato paste, thyme, parsley flakes, duck and two cups reserved bean liquid. Mix well and heat for 3 minutes.

Layer the bean mixture and sausage mixture alternately in a large casserole. Bake in the oven for 1 hour.

SOAK: overnight | **PREP TIME:** 10 minutes | **COOK TIME:** 2 1/2 hours | **SERVES:** 6 to 8

KATIE'S GOOSE

1 medium goose

4 to 5 quarts cold water

4 to 6 Tablespoons salt

2 pounds lean beef

1 pound cracked beef bones

1 pound carrots, peeled and chopped

1 pound turnips, quartered

1 pound leeks, sliced

Garlic

Black pepper

Bay leaf

Thyme

1 cup white wine

French bread

Remove the skin of the goose, wash and dry. Split the goose into halves. Using a large pot with a tight-fitting lid, pour in the water and dissolve the salt. Add the goose halves, the beef cut into squares and the cracked beef bones. If the water doesn't cover all the meat, add more water and salt. Very slowly increase the temperature and remove the "scum" from the surface of the water as often as needed; the "scum" forms before liquid comes to a boil. Allow the mixture to boil and add the carrots, turnips, leeks and a little garlic. Season with the pepper, a bay leaf and a pinch of thyme. Pour in the wine. Cover tightly, reduce heat to a low simmer and cook for 4 hours. Remove the goose, beef and vegetables and drain well; keep warm. Remove all the bones and bits of bones from the liquid in the pot. On large plates, place some of each vegetable on thick pieces of the French bread. Pour the liquid over all. Carve the goose and serve with the beef.

PREP TIME: 30 minutes | **COOK TIME:** 4 1/2 hours | **SERVES:** 8 to 12

HUNTING TIP

When hunting ducks in an area that has both flooded timber and fields, follow the old-timer's advice and hunt the timber when it's sunny and fields when it's cloudy.

DUCK MEAT FOR JAMBALAYA

2 large ducks

1 Tablespoon salt

1 Tablespoon pepper

1 onion, quartered

2 ribs celery, chopped

1 bay leaf

In a large pot, cook the ducks in water seasoned with salt, pepper, onion, celery and bay leaf for about 1 1/2 hours, or until tender. Remove the ducks and cool. Remove the meat from the bone and cut into bite-size pieces.

PREP TIME: 5 minutes | **COOK TIME:** 1 1/2 hours

DUCK JAMBALAYA

3 Tablespoons bacon grease

3 Tablespoons flour

2 medium onions, chopped

1 cup green onions, chopped

2 Tablespoons fresh parsley, chopped

1 cup celery, chopped

1 cup green pepper, chopped

2 cloves garlic, minced

2 cups chicken stock

1 cup rice

2 teaspoons salt

1/2 teaspoon cayenne

4 cups duck meat for jambalaya (recipe on page 92)

In a large heavy pot, heat the bacon grease and gradually add the flour, stirring constantly until the roux is dark brown. Add the onions, parsley, celery, green pepper and garlic. Cook until soft. Add the chicken stock, a cup or so of water, rice, salt, cayenne and duck meat. Bring to a boil; then lower heat as much as possible. Cook 1 hour, tightly covered. Stir occasionally. When the rice is done, remove the cover and cook a few more minutes so rice will steam dry.

PREP TIME: 20 minutes | **COOK TIME:** 1 1/2 hours | **SERVES:** 4 to 6

CROCK-POT DUCK

2 ducks

Salt and pepper

Garlic powder

Salad oil

1 (10 3/4 oz.) can condensed cream of mushroom soup

1 soup can of milk

1 onion, cut in chunks

1 (4 oz.) can mushrooms

Cut up the birds and marinate for 8 hours in cold water in the refrigerator. Season the birds with salt, pepper and plenty of garlic powder. Brown them in the oil. Place in a Crock-Pot with soup, milk, onion and mushrooms. Cook for 6 to 8 hours.

MARINATE: 8 hours | **PREP TIME:** 10 minutes | **COOK TIME:** 6 to 8 hours | **SERVES:** 4 to 6

HUNTING TIP *by Harold Knight*

To be a successful turkey hunter, learn to use a mouth blown call as well as a friction type call. Mastering many types of calls allows you to sound like more than one turkey and offers a variety of sounds which is important throughout the turkey season.

GRILLED WILD TURKEY STRIPS

Wild turkey, cut in strips 1" thick

1 stick butter, melted

3 Tablespoons lemon juice

Salt and pepper

Warm the butter and mix in the lemon juice, salt and pepper to taste. Baste the turkey strips and place on a greased grill about 6" above hot coals (or high heat on a gas grill). Grill for 5 or 6 minutes on each side, basting from time to time.

PREP TIME: 10 minutes | COOK TIME: 15 minutes | SERVES: 8

TURKEY WRAPS

1 cup creamy Caesar dressing

4 (12") flour tortillas

12 leaves romaine lettuce

2 cups cooked wild turkey, chopped

1 (7 oz.) jar drained roasted red peppers

1/4 cup grated Parmesan cheese

Spread 2 to 3 Tablespoons of Caesar dressing over the surface of each tortilla. Place 3 lettuce leaves on each tortilla and press them into the dressing. Place the turkey and roasted red peppers equally on one half of each tortilla. Sprinkle the Parmesan cheese over the top, and roll each tightly, starting with the turkey side. Wrap individually and refrigerate for 1 hour. Cut each wrap to size before serving.

PREP TIME: 20 minutes + 1 hour | **SERVES:** 4

JUICY GOOSE

1 (4- to 5-pound) goose

1/2 cup orange juice

1/2 cup dry white wine

1/4 cup butter

1 Tablespoon lemon juice

1 teaspoon basil

1/8 teaspoon orange peel

1/4 teaspoon dry mustard

Parsley sprigs

Orange wedges

Preheat the oven to 450°.

Heat the orange juice, wine, butter, lemon juice, basil, orange peel and dry mustard in a small pan. Place the goose in a roasting pan and pour a little of the hot orange sauce over the goose. Roast in the oven for 45 minutes, basting every 10 minutes with the sauce. Place the goose on a platter and garnish with parsley sprigs and orange wedges. Carve the breast into thin slices and serve, ladling a little of the remaining sauce over the slices.

PREP TIME: 10 minutes | **COOK TIME:** 1 hour | **SERVES:** 8 to 10

WILD TURKEY CASSEROLE

submitted by HAROLD KNIGHT

3 Tablespoons olive oil

2 large carrots, peeled and diced

3 celery ribs, thinly sliced

1 medium onion, minced

5 garlic cloves, minced

3 (15 oz.) cans drained white kidney beans or Great Northern beans

1 (6 oz.) can tomato sauce

2 to 3 cups wild turkey, cooked and cut in 1 1/2" pieces

3/4 pound smoked turkey sausage, cut in 1/2" thick slices

1 1/2 cups canned or homemade chicken or turkey broth

1/2 teaspoon dried thyme leaves

Pinch of ground cloves

Salt and pepper

1 cup coarse white bread crumbs

1/2 cup fresh parsley, minced

Preheat the oven to 350°.

Heat 1 1/2 Tablespoons of the olive oil over medium-high heat in a Dutch oven or ovenproof casserole dish. Add the carrots, celery, onion and 3 of the minced garlic cloves. Sauté until softened, 5 to 7 minutes. Remove from the heat and add the beans, tomato sauce, turkey and smoked sausage. Pour in the broth and stir to combine all the ingredients thoroughly. Season with thyme, cloves, salt and pepper. Cover the Dutch oven or casserole and bake in the oven for 45 minutes. Mix bread crumbs, parsley, the remaining garlic and the remaining 1 1/2 Tablespoons olive oil. Uncover the casserole and sprinkle the crumb mixture over the top. Continue baking, uncovered, until the crumbs are lightly browned and the casserole is bubbling, about 20 minutes more.

PREP TIME: 30 minutes | **COOK TIME:** 1 1/2 hours | **SERVES:** 6 to 8

BROILED TURKEY TERIYAKI

1/2 cup soy sauce

1/4 cup sake, dry vermouth or sherry

2 Tablespoons brown sugar

1 Tablespoon fresh ginger root, finely grated

2 cloves garlic, finely grated

Black pepper (optional)

1 to 2 pounds turkey strips, cut 1" thick

Cooked rice

Asian stir-fried vegetables (cooked separately)

Mix the soy sauce, sake, brown sugar, ginger root and garlic. Add the black pepper to taste (note it is not a traditional teriyaki ingredient). Put the turkey strips into a non-metallic container and pour the marinade over them. Stir the strips to coat all sides and marinate in the refrigerator for 1 to 2 hours.

Preheat the broiler.

Broil the turkey strips for about 5 minutes on each side, basting two or three times with the leftover marinade. Test for doneness. Serve with rice and Asian stir-fried vegetables.

PREP TIME: 15 minutes | **MARINATE:** 1 to 2 hours | **COOK TIME:** 10 minutes | **SERVES:** 4 to 8

HUNTING TIP

Get out before the season and check out your turkey hunting area. A few walks in the woods will provide valuable insight into where the turkeys are staging. Fresh scratching in the leaves is the most common late winter/early spring sign.

HONEY-BAKED TURKEY

1 (10- to 12-pound) turkey

6 Tablespoons honey

1 teaspoon salt

1 teaspoon coarse black pepper

Stuffing (see SIDES chapter, page 111)

3/4 cup onion, chopped

2 cups white wine

1/2 cup chicken broth

1 teaspoon parsley flakes

1 stick butter, melted

1 teaspoon Creole seasoning

Preheat the oven to 325°.

Warm the honey and brush the turkey with it; then season turkey with salt and pepper. Place on a rack in a large baking pan. Place the stuffing inside the turkey. Mix the onion, wine, broth and parsley; then add the butter and Creole seasoning. Baste the bird with the wine mixture. Place in the oven and roast for 4 hours, basting occasionally with the wine mixture.

PREP TIME: 10 minutes | **COOK TIME:** 4 1/2 hours | **SERVES:** 10 to 15

BEER CAN TURKEY

1 turkey (reserve gizzard)

1 can beer

Aluminum pie plate

Vegetable oil

Salt and pepper

Paprika

Garlic

Herbs of choice

Prepare a hot grill (or preheat an oven to 400°).

Wash an unopened can of beer. Open the top, and punch holes around the top of the beer can. Pour one-third of the beer into a pie plate. Wash the turkey and gizzard. Set the gizzard aside and put the turkey, rubbed with oil, in the pie plate. Put the salt, pepper, paprika and garlic (to taste) in the beer can. Put the gizzard over the big hole in the beer can, and place the can inside the bird. Put the turkey on the grill (or in the oven) and cook for 1 1/4 hours.

PREP TIME: 15 minutes | **COOK TIME:** 1 hour and 15 minutes | **SERVES:** 6 to 8

DUCK GUMBO

submitted by KELLY POWERS

6 to 8 duck breasts
2 quarts water
1/2 stick margarine
1 cup flour
1 1/2 cups celery, chopped
2 large bell peppers, chopped
3 cloves garlic, minced
1 bunch green onions, chopped
1 teaspoon parsley
1 teaspoon oregano
1 teaspoon thyme
2 Tablespoons salt
1 Tablespoon black pepper
1 teaspoon red pepper

Wash and prepare duck breasts. Place them in a Crock Pot in 2 quarts of water and cook for 2 1/2 hours. Remove, reserving stock and chop duck breasts into bite size pieces.

In a large pot, melt the butter and slowly add the flour, stirring constantly to make a roux. You may need to add some water to keep it in a gravy-like consistency. Add about 2 quarts of the duck stock from the Crock Pot. Bring to a boil. Then add the chopped duck breasts, celery, bell peppers, garlic, green onions, parsley, oregano, thyme, salt, black pepper and red pepper. Lower heat and simmer for 2 hours.

Serve in bowls over rice.

PREP TIME: 20 minutes | **COOK TIME:** 4 horus and 30 minutes | **SERVES:** 8 to 10

HERB BAKED CATFISH: page 49

MIKE'S DUCK GUMBO: page 80

BASS STUFFED MUSHROOM CAPS: page 72

TROUT NANCY: page 62

VENISON STUFFED GRAPE LEAVES: page 21

VENISON AND RICE CASSEROLE: page 26

PHEASANT PASTA: page 83

DUCK BREAST SALAD: page 37

TURKEY WRAPS: page 96

GRILLED SNAPPER: page 56

NOT-SO-SPICY FRIED FISH: page 40

VENISON STOGANOFF: page 33

SIDE DISHES

CRYSTAL GINGER SWEET POTATOES

4 medium-size sweet potatoes

3 Tablespoons butter

1/4 cup crystallized ginger, cut into small pieces

1/4 cup orange juice

1/4 cup brown sugar, firmly packed

Preheat the oven to 375°.

Peel and boil the sweet potatoes until tender but firm; cut into slices. Arrange a layer of the sliced potatoes in a buttered casserole. Dot with the butter and sprinkle with the ginger. Repeat with the next layer. Pour the orange juice over the potatoes and sprinkle with the brown sugar. Bake uncovered in the oven for 45 minutes. Baste occasionally to keep moist.

PREP TIME: 15 minutes | **COOK TIME:** 1 hour | **SERVES:** 6

MINTED APPLE RINGS

1 cup sugar

2 1/4 cups water

1/4 teaspoon green food coloring

2 tart, medium-size apples (not peeled), sliced

2 teaspoons mint flavoring

Mix the sugar, water and food coloring in a heavy skillet. Boil for 5 minutes to form a syrup. Slice the apples crosswise about 1/4" thick. Do not core the apples, but remove the seeds. Add the mint flavoring to the syrup and place the apple slices in the syrup. Boil over medium heat for 15 to 20 minutes, or until the apples become transparent. Turn the slices occasionally and baste with the syrup. Remove the slices from the syrup and cool before serving.

PREP TIME: 10 minutes | **COOK TIME:** 30 minutes | **SERVES:** 2 to 4

HOT DEVILED POTATOES

2 cups mashed potatoes

1/4 cup nonfat sour cream or yogurt

2 teaspoons prepared mustard

1/4 teaspoon salt

1/4 teaspoon sugar

2 Tablespoons green onion, chopped

Paprika

Prepare the potatoes (if instant, according to package directions), or warm leftover potatoes. Heat the sour cream in a medium saucepan, being careful not to boil. Add the mustard, salt and sugar, and blend. Stir the sour cream mixture into the hot potatoes. Add the onion and blend. Serve, sprinkled with the paprika.

PREP TIME: 10 minutes | COOK TIME: 20 minutes | SERVES: 4

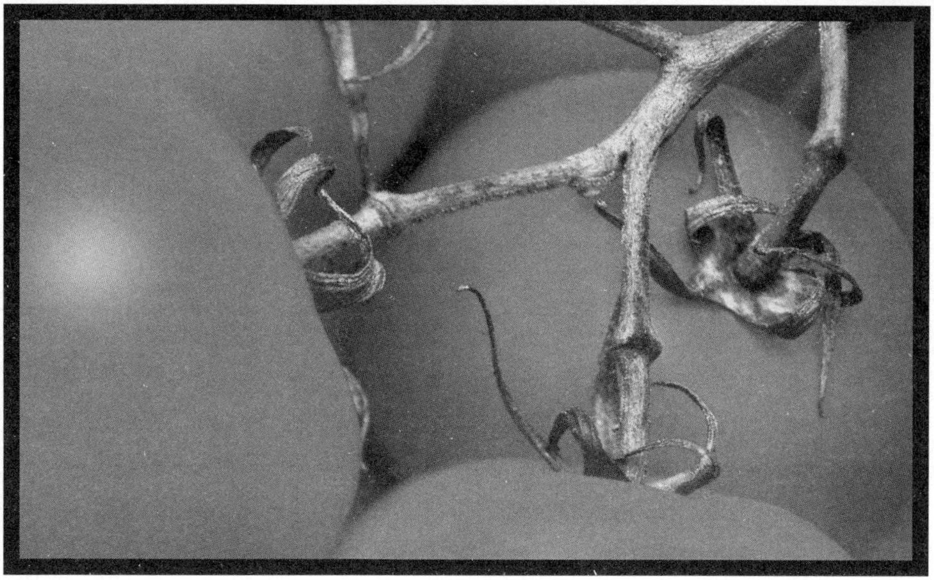

TOMATO PIE

1 (9") piecrust, unbaked

2 to 4 tomatoes

Seasoned salt

1/4 teaspoon basil

1/4 cup fresh chives, chopped

1/4 cup mayonnaise

1 cup cheddar cheese

Preheat the oven to 425°.

Cook the piecrust for 5 minutes. Remove and reduce oven temperature to 400°.

Cut the tomatoes in thick slices to cover the bottom of the pie crust; sprinkle with seasoned salt. Sprinkle the basil and chives over the tomatoes. Mix the mayonnaise with the cheese and spread over the top to seal the tomatoes. Put the pie in the oven and bake for 30 to 35 minutes.

PREP TIME: 10 minutes | **COOK TIME:** 40 minutes | **SERVES:** 8

WILD RICE WITH LEEKS AND MUSHROOMS

3 cups water

1 1/4 cups wild rice

3 1/4 cups fat-free chicken broth

1 Tablespoon olive oil

3 leeks, chopped

1/4 cup sliced mushrooms

1/4 teaspoon ground black pepper

In a large saucepan, combine the water and rice. Bring to a boil over high heat. Cover, remove from the heat, and let stand for 20 minutes. Drain rice well and return to the pan. Add 3 cups of the broth. Bring to a boil over medium-high heat. Stir, cover, reduce the heat and simmer for 25 minutes, or until the rice is just tender and the liquid has been absorbed. While the rice is cooking, warm the oil in a large nonstick skillet over medium heat. Add the leeks and sauté for 3 minutes. Add the mushrooms and sauté for 3 minutes. Add the pepper and the remaining 1/4 cup broth. Cover and simmer for 5 minutes. When the rice is done, add the vegetable mixture to the rice pan and mix well.

PREP TIME: 10 minutes | **COOK TIME:** 1 hour | **SERVES:** 8

RICE CASSEROLE

1 cup cooked rice

4 teaspoons melted margarine

2 cups chicken broth

1/4 cup almonds, slivered

1/4 cup parsley, chopped

1/4 cup green onions, chopped

1/4 cup carrots, chopped

1/4 cup celery, chopped

Preheat the oven to 350°.

Coat the rice with melted margarine. Place in a casserole and add the chicken broth. Bake uncovered for 40 minutes. Stir in the almonds, parsley, green onions, carrots and celery. Cook 15 minutes longer.

PREP TIME: 20 minutes | **COOK TIME:** 1 hour | **SERVES:** 4

SWEET POTATO ROLLS

1 cup mashed sweet potatoes

3 Tablespoons low-fat margarine, melted

1 package rapid rise yeast

1 1/4 cups warm water (110° to 115°)

1 large egg

1 teaspoon light salt

3 Tablespoons sugar

5 cups all purpose flour

Preheat the oven to 425°.

Blend the potatoes with melted margarine. Dissolve the yeast in 1/4 cup warm water. Combine the potatoes with the egg, salt, sugar and yeast mixture. Add flour alternately with the remaining 1/4 cup water, mixing until well combined. Turn onto a well-floured board and knead. Place in a bowl coated with nonstick spray. Cover and allow to rise 1 hour in a warm place. Divide the dough into 24 pieces and form into rolls. Place on a baking sheet coated with nonstick spray and let rise in a warm place for 30 minutes or until doubled in size.

Bake until done, 20 to 30 minutes.

PREP TIME: 2 hours | **COOK TIME:** 30 minutes | **YIELD:** 24 rolls

SAUSAGE/PECAN STUFFING

1 cup celery, chopped

1/4 to 1 cup onion, chopped

1/4 cup bell pepper, chopped

1 stick margarine

8 cups corn bread, crumbled

5 cups white bread, cubed, or 3 cups bread crumbs, toasted

5 cups canned chicken broth

1/4 pound pork sausage

Giblets from wild turkey or chicken, finely chopped (optional)

1/4 teaspoon salt

1/4 Tablespoon black pepper

4 eggs, slightly beaten

1 cup pecans, chopped

Preheat the oven to 325°.

In a heavy skillet, cook the celery, onion and bell pepper in margarine until tender. Place the corn bread and cubes or crumbs in a large bowl; add heated chicken broth and sautéed vegetables, mixing well. Cook the sausage until browned, adding giblets when almost done. Add to the bread mixture the seasonings, eggs and chopped pecans. Toss lightly to mix well. Put the stuffing in a 13 x 9 x 2" pan; do not cover. Bake for 45 minutes.

PREP TIME: 25 minutes | **COOK TIME:** 1 hour | **SERVES:** 15 to 20

CLASSIC BREAD STUFFING

1/4 cup unsalted butter

2 medium onions, chopped

3 medium celery ribs, chopped

1/4 cup celery leaves (from inner ribs), chopped

1 pound white bread (cut in 1/4" cubes), dried, or 10 cups plain bread croutons

1/4 cup fresh parsley, chopped

2 teaspoons poultry seasoning

1 1/4 teaspoons salt

1/4 teaspoon freshly ground pepper

1 1/4 to 2 cups turkey or chicken broth, as needed

If you are not planning to stuff your turkey with this stuffing, preheat the oven to 325°.

In a large skillet, melt the butter over medium heat. Add the onions, celery and celery leaves. Cook, stirring often, until the onions are golden, about 8 minutes. Scrape the vegetables and butter into a large bowl. Mix in the bread cubes or croutons, parsley, poultry seasoning, salt and pepper. Gradually stir in about 1 1/4 cups broth, until the stuffing is evenly moistened but not soggy. Use the mixture as a stuffing or place in a lightly buttered casserole, drizzle with 1/4 cup broth, cover, and bake for 30 to 40 minutes.

PREP TIME: 20 minutes | **COOK TIME:** 1 hour | **SERVES:** 8 to 10

APPLE/RAISIN WHOLE WHEAT STUFFING

12 cups whole wheat bread, cubed

1 1/4 cups raisins

4 apples (not peeled), chopped

1 1/4 cups onion, finely chopped

4 cups celery, thinly sliced

3 eggs (or egg whites)

1 cup walnuts or pecans, chopped

4 Tablespoons margarine, melted

2 1/4 cups chicken broth

1/4 teaspoon freshly ground black pepper

If you are not planning to stuff your turkey with this mixture, preheat the oven to 325°.

If the bread is not stale, spread the slices out on a rack or counter for half a day to dry and then cut into cubes. Combine the bread cubes with raisins, apples, onion, celery, eggs, walnuts or pecans, margarine, chicken broth and black pepper. Stuff the turkey or bake in a covered oven-proof dish for about 40 minutes at 325°.

Note:

An alternate cooking method is to spoon the stuffing into a Crock-Pot and cook on high for 2 hours; then cook on low for 4 hours.

PREP TIME: 20 minutes | **COOK TIME:** 40 minutes | **SERVES:** 12

ARCHERY ELK HUNTING *by Ken Cook*

One of my favorite hunting trips is for elk during their bugling season. Normally, this means bowhunting, which is, again, my favorite. It is best to think of a bull elk just like a turkey gobbler. He really does not want to fight another bull, but rather is looking for female companionship. I use a bull bugle to first locate a target bull by getting him to bugle a response. Then, after moving into a better strategic position, down wind of the animal, I make cow elk sounds. The bull is much more likely to approach these mews and chirps of a lonesome cow than he would be a challenging bull. Keep in mind, the wind is a very important factor in this scenario. The bull, upon his approach, will most likely swing toward the downwind side of your position to scent check his potential companion. Have an open shooting lane that provides a shooting opportunity before the bull gets completely downwind of your position. This provides the best opportunity for a broadside shot. You may have to adjust your position to acquire this optimum position as the bull approaches, but making noise is okay with elk because they make a lot of noise as they move normally through their woods.

HOECAKES

4 cups cornmeal

1 onion, chopped

About 1 pint buttermilk

Corn oil for frying

In a medium bowl, mix the cornmeal, onion and enough buttermilk to make a batter. Using a large skillet, heat a small amount of oil and dip out the batter to make 4 cakes at a time. Fry until one side is brown; then turn over and cook the other side. Serve hot.

PREP TIME: 15 minutes | **COOK TIME:** 20 minutes | **YIELDS:** 20 to 24 cakes

SOUTHERN CORN BREAD

1 cup yellow cornmeal

1/4 teaspoon salt

1 cup flour

4 teaspoons baking powder

1 medium egg, slightly beaten

1 cup skim milk

Preheat the oven to 425°.

Mix the cornmeal, salt, flour and baking powder. Add the egg and milk, and mix well. Pour into a 12 x 8" pan sprayed with nonstick spray. Bake in the oven for 25 minutes. Cut into 12 squares.

PREP TIME: 10 minutes | **COOK TIME:** 30 minutes | **SERVES:** 12

JALAPEÑO HUSH PUPPIES

1 1/4 cups cornmeal

1/4 cup flour

2 1/4 Tablespoons baking powder

1 1/4 Tablespoons salt

1/4 Tablespoon pepper

1/4 cup onion, finely chopped

1 cup milk

1 egg, beaten

3 Tablespoons oil

1/4 cup jalapeño peppers, finely chopped

Vegetable oil

Combine the cornmeal, flour, baking powder, salt, pepper, onion, milk, egg, oil and peppers. Stir until blended. Using a spoon or fork, drop into deep, hot oil. Dip the spoon or fork into hot oil each time and the batter will drop off more easily. Fry until golden, turning once during cooking. Drain.

PREP TIME: 15 minutes | **COOK TIME:** 20 minutes | **SERVES:** 4 to 6

HUSH PUPPIES

1 cup self-rising flour

1 cup self-rising cornmeal

1/4 teaspoon baking powder

1/4 teaspoon baking soda

2 Tablespoons sugar

1 egg

2 large onions, finely chopped

1/4 cup buttermilk

Vegetable oil

Mix the flour, cornmeal, baking powder, baking soda, sugar, egg, onions and buttermilk well. Set the bowl aside, cover, and let the mixture rise (it won't be a huge rise, but it does lift a bit). Spoon a ball of the mixture and gently place it into hot oil. The hush puppies will brown beautifully; when they are golden brown, take them out and place them on a paper towel to soak up any extra oil.

PREP TIME: 10 minutes | **COOK TIME:** 20 minutes | **SERVES:** 4 to 6

CORN BREAD/SAUSAGE STUFFING

1 pan corn bread, made from a mix

1/4 pound turkey sausage (with casings removed)

1 Tablespoon light margarine

2 cups onions, chopped

1 1/4 cups celery, chopped

2 teaspoons dried sage

1 teaspoon dried marjoram

1 teaspoon dried rosemary, crumbled

1/4 cup white cooking wine

1/4 cup green onions, sliced

1/4 cup fat-free egg substitute

1 cup reduced-fat chicken broth

Preheat the oven to 375°.

Crumble the corn bread into a large, shallow pan. Bake in the oven, stirring often, until crumbs are golden brown, 15 to 20 minutes. Remove and reduce oven temperature to 325°.

Break up the sausage and cook over medium-high heat in a nonstick skillet until browned and cooked through, 5 to 7 minutes. Transfer to a bowl. Add the margarine to the skillet and heat until melted. Add the onions and celery. Cook, stirring often, until vegetables are tender, 4 to 5 minutes. Add the sage, marjoram and rosemary. Cook, stirring constantly for 2 minutes. Add the vegetable mixture to the sausage. Mix in the corn bread, wine, onions and egg substitute. Coat a 3 quart casserole with nonstick spray. Spoon the stuffing into the casserole and drizzle with the broth. Cover and bake at 325° for 30 minutes. Uncover and bake until golden, 20 to 30 minutes.

PREP TIME: 15 minutes | COOK TIME: 1 hour 30 minutes | SERVES: 8

WILD TURKEY STUFFING

Wild turkey gizzard, liver and heart

1 large loaf bread, sliced

1/4 cup celery, chopped

2 large white onions, peeled

1/4 cup butter

2 1/4 Tablespoons shortening

2 cups pecans, chopped

Salt and pepper

Boil the gizzard, liver and heart in water until very tender. Cut all the gristle off the gizzard. Save the broth. Toast each slice of bread well on both sides. Grind separately the toasted bread, celery, onions and turkey giblets; reserve in separate dishes. In a large frying pan, sauté the onions in butter and shortening. Add the celery and giblets. Sprinkle in the toast crumbs and pecans. Salt and pepper to taste. Add just enough broth to make a lightly moist stuffing.

PREP TIME: 20 minutes | **COOK TIME:** 30 minutes | **SERVES:** 12 to 15

POACHED APPLES

5 apples
1 cup sugar
2 cups water
1/4 teaspoon salt
5 to 6 drops red food coloring
1/2 teaspoon cinnamon extract
1/4 teaspoon nutmeg extract
1 teaspoon vanilla extract

Pare the apples and cut them in half crosswise. Pick out the seeds, but do not core. Combine the sugar, water, salt, food coloring, cinnamon extract, nutmeg extract and vanilla in a large skillet and bring to a boil to make a syrup. Stir in the apples and simmer until tender, watching carefully, so they will not get too tender all at once.

Note:

If nutmeg and cinnamon flavoring extracts are not obtainable, use the same amounts of the dry spice, mixing with the 1 cup sugar before adding to the water.

PREP TIME: 15 minutes | **COOK TIME:** 15 minutes | **SERVES:** 10

STUFFED SQUASH

2 yellow crookneck squash, sliced in half lengthwise

8 strips bacon, cooked and crumbled

1/4 cup bread crumbs

1/4 cup sour cream

Seasoned salt

Pepper

4 slices Swiss cheese

Preheat the oven to broil.

Place the squash cut side down in a microwaveable dish. Microwave on high for 3 minutes, turning after 1 1/4 minutes. Check to make sure the seeded part of the squash is soft. After the squash has cooled slightly, scoop out the fleshy part, reserving the shells, and mix the squash with the bacon, bread crumbs, sour cream, salt and pepper. Put the mixture back into the squash boats and top with Swiss cheese. Put under the broiler until the cheese has browned.

PREP TIME: 10 minutes | COOK TIME: 10 minutes | SERVES: 4

CURRIED RICE

1 Tablespoon onion, minced

2 Tablespoons butter or margarine

Curry powder, to taste

1/4 teaspoon salt

1/4 teaspoon pepper

3 cups hot, cooked rice

1/4 cup almonds, slivered and toasted

1/4 cup pimiento-stuffed olives or pitted ripe olives, chopped

In a small skillet, cook and stir the onion in the butter until the onion is tender. Stir in the curry powder, salt and pepper. Mix into the hot rice. Sprinkle the almonds and olives over the rice.

PREP TIME: 20 minutes | COOK TIME: 15 minutes | SERVES: 6

CURRIED BAKED FRUIT

1 (24 oz.) can pear halves

1 (20 oz.) can pineapple chunks

1 (24 oz.) can peach halves

1/4 cup maraschino cherries, sliced

1/4 cup butter or margarine

2 teaspoons curry powder

1/4 cup light brown sugar

Preheat the oven to 325°.

Drain the pear halves, pineapple chunks, peach halves and maraschino cherries and place in a casserole dish. Melt the butter in a saucepan and add the curry powder and sugar. Mix well. Pour over the fruit and bake uncovered in the oven for 1 hour.

PREP TIME: 15 minutes | **COOK TIME:** 1 hour | **SERVES:** 6 to 8

SOUTHWEST BAKED BEANS

1 pound ground beef

1/4 cup honey

1/4 cup ketchup

1 Tablespoon cider vinegar

1 teaspoon chili powder

1 teaspoon salt

1 (32 oz.) can black beans or kidney beans, rinsed

1 (12 oz.) can whole kernel corn, drained

1 (4 oz.) can chopped green chilies, drained, or 1 large jalapeño, seeded and chopped

1/4 cup onion, chopped

2 Tablespoons cilantro, chopped

Red bell pepper rings

Cilantro sprigs

Preheat the oven to 350°.

Brown and drain the ground beef. In a 1 1/4 quart casserole, combine the honey, ketchup, vinegar, chili powder, salt, beans, corn, green chilies, onion and chopped cilantro. Add the browned ground beef. Cover and bake in the oven for 45 minutes, stirring occasionally. Arrange the bell pepper rings over the top, re-cover, and continue baking for 15 minutes. Garnish with the cilantro sprigs.

PREP TIME: 15 minutes | COOK TIME: 1 hour | SERVES: 6

WATERFOWL HABITS IN EXTREME WEATHER CONDITIONS *by Kelly Powers*

Pay special attention to waterfowl's habits in extreme weather conditions and use such information to alter your hunting strategies to become more efficient. For example; when the temperature is extremely cold, and everything is frozen solid, the birds are generally not very active because long flights burn too much vital energy. To survive, they must conserve their reserves as much as possible. During these times, they must consume foods high in protein; thus, pay keen attention to the available natural food sources in the area which you hunt. When the temperature inevitably warms, they take longer flights and actively scour for open splash water to feed in. By spending more time scouting, your success in the field will greatly increase.

OLD FASHIONED CHILI

8 pounds ground round beef
3 packages mild chili seasoning
12 (16 oz.) cans chili-hot beans
2 medium onions, chopped
6 (16 oz.) cans stewed tomatoes
2 (8 oz.) cans mushrooms

Brown the ground beef. Add the chili seasoning, beans, onions, tomatoes and mushrooms. Cook for 30 minutes, stirring occasionally.

Note:

This recipe is perfect for a party or afternoon with several friends dropping by. If you don't eat it all you can refrigerate it for reheating later in the week.

PREP TIME: 15 minutes | **COOK TIME:** 30 minutes | **SERVES:** 25 to 30

GRANNY'S SLAW

1 medium head cabbage, shredded

2 Tablespoons fresh parsley, chopped

1 cup carrots, shredded

1 cup green pepper, finely chopped

1/4 cup green onion, chopped

3 Tablespoons vinegar

1 cup mayonnaise

1 Tablespoon mustard

Dash of garlic powder

Salt and pepper

Dash of cayenne

Combine the cabbage, parsley, carrots, green pepper and onion in a large bowl. Whisk together the vinegar, mayonnaise, mustard, garlic powder, salt, pepper and cayenne in a smaller bowl and pour over the cabbage mixture, stirring to coat well. Cover and refrigerate 2 to 3 hours before serving. Stir again before serving.

PREP TIME: 30 minutes | **CHILL:** 2 to 3 hours | **SERVES:** 6 to 8

WHITE CHILI

2 pounds ground turkey
2 medium white onions, chopped
2 Tablespoons garlic, minced
2 teaspoons oregano
4 Tablespoons cumin
2 (4 oz.) jars green chilies, chopped
3 (7 oz.) cans green tomatillo salsa or salsa verde
3 (16 oz.) cans white beans, rinsed and drained
2 (14 1/2 oz.) cans chicken broth
Nacho chips
Cheddar cheese, shredded
Green onions, chopped

Sauté the ground turkey with the onions, garlic, oregano, cumin and chilies until browned; drain the fat. Remove mixture to a large pot. Add the salsa, beans and chicken broth. Cook for 45 minutes to 1 hour to blend the flavors. Serve with Nacho chips, shredded cheddar cheese and chopped green onions.

PREP TIME: 15 minutes | COOK TIME: 1 hour 15 minutes | SERVES: 8

CRANBERRY BEETS

1 cup water

1 cup sugar

2 cups raw cranberries

1 teaspoon cornstarch

1 Tablespoon cold water

1 (16 oz.) can cubed beets

Mix the water and sugar and boil for 5 minutes. Add the washed cranberries and cook without stirring until the cranberries pop open, about 5 minutes. Drain the juice from the cranberries and return the juice to the heat. Mix the cornstarch with the cold water to make a smooth paste. Add paste to the juice and cook until clear and thickened, about 3 to 4 minutes. Add the berries and the drained beets to the thickened juice. Heat all together until hot.

Note: This dish can be served hot or cold.

PREP TIME: 5 minutes | COOK TIME: 20 minutes | SERVES: 8

SUMMER CORN

4 ears sweet corn

2 yellow squash, sliced

1 medium onion, chopped

Salt and pepper, to taste

Water (optional)

1/4 cup butter

In a large bowl, cut the corn from the cob, scraping the cob to get the milk. Add the squash, onion, salt and pepper. If the mixture seems dry, add the water, 1 Tablespoon at a time, to moisten – you will want some liquid to form in the bottom of the bowl. Melt the butter in a large skillet. Add the corn mixture. Cook, covered, over medium heat until squash and onions are tender, about 10 to 15 minutes. Stir occasionally. Uncover, increase the heat to medium-high, and stir frequently until lightly browned. If the mixture appears sticky, you can add more butter or water. Serve immediately.

PREP TIME: 15 minutes | **COOK TIME:** 30 minutes | **SERVES:** 4

CABBAGE ROLLS WITH SOUR CREAM SAUCE

1 pound ground turkey sausage

1/4 cup onions, diced

1/4 cup celery, diced

1 cup cooked rice

1 teaspoon prepared horseradish

1 teaspoon prepared brown mustard

1/4 cup fat-free egg substitute

8 large cabbage leaves

1/4 cup tomato sauce

1/4 cup water

1 cup nonfat sour cream

Preheat the oven to 350°.

Coat a large skillet with nonstick spray. Warm over low heat and sauté the sausage and onions until lightly browned. Remove from the heat and add the celery, rice, horseradish, mustard and egg substitute. Fill a 3 quart saucepan with water and bring it to a boil. Add the cabbage and cook for 3 minutes. Drain the cabbage in a colander. Divide the meat mixture among the cabbage leaves. Roll up the leaves and fasten with toothpicks. Coat a 7 x 11" baking dish with nonstick spray and add the rolled cabbage leaves. Pour the tomato sauce, mixed with the 1/4 cup water, over the rolls. Cover and bake for 30 minutes. Using a slotted spoon, transfer the cabbage rolls to a platter. Add the sour cream to the liquid in the baking dish and whisk to combine. Serve over the cabbage rolls.

PREP TIME: 20 minutes | **COOK TIME:** 45 minutes | **SERVES:** 8

CHEDDAR POTATO SALAD

12 cups cooked potatoes, diced

2 cups celery, sliced

8 hard-cooked eggs, chopped

4 cups sharp cheddar cheese, shredded

1/4 cup green onions, sliced

2 cups salad dressing

1 Tablespoon prepared mustard

1 Tablespoon salt

1/4 teaspoon pepper

Combine the potatoes, celery, eggs, cheese and onions; mix lightly. In a separate bowl, combine the salad dressing, mustard and seasonings; mix lightly. Pour the dressing over the potato mixture and mix gently. Chill for 1 hour before serving.

PREP TIME: 30 minutes | **CHILL:** 1 hour | **SERVES:** 20 to 22

BOAT BLIND BASICS

by Steve McCadams

Boat blinds offer hunters mobility. And, since the ducks move around and change flight patterns from time to time, you should too.

Today's camouflage patterns offer hunters a great chance to blend into their surroundings and Triton has waterfowlers in mind with its various models and lengths. From deep in the swamp where flooded timber is the norm, to marsh grass on the edge of lakes and rivers, there's a model and pattern that fits your needs.

Three words best describe the criteria for a successful boat blind hunt; those would be "location-location-location."

In waterfowling, the wind giveth and it taketh away. Choosing your spot in the predawn hours can be challenging and with a boat blind you have the flexibility to move during the day.

However, pay close attention to wind direction and setup where the ducks will have an open approach to your decoy spread. Their final approach needs to be free of hurdles so don't try to make them swing low over bushes and trees.

Set your decoys so the ducks can see them but keep the wind direction in mind. It's a good idea to put the wind either at your back or parallel to the boat blind. This way, ducks will either come directly in front of you or you'll have them pass like a parade where everyone can shoot.

Scouting out areas and finding where the ducks are rafting can put you in the driver's seat. Even when you scare birds out of an area, chances are they'll return if you get set up quickly or lay out your strategy for the next morning.

Boat blinds also enable you to hunt finicky, late season ducks that aren't likely to move around much or work permanent blinds. If they've been in the area for a spell then they've pretty much learned the territory and likely avoid high use areas of hunting pressure.

Your mobile blind will put the element of surprise on your side.

I would also recommend using magnum size decoys as they're more conspicuous and you don't have to toss out (and pick up) as many. Using some movement in the spread is good, too, ranging from motion wing models to the wobble style that create ripples and mimic feeding ducks.

DUTCH POTATO SALAD

6 oz. mild cheddar or Monterey Jack cheese
2 1/2 pounds red potatoes
5 slices bacon, cooked and crumbled
1/2 cup green onions, sliced
1 1/2 cups mayonnaise
1/2 cup light cream
1/4 cup mustard
1/2 teaspoon pepper

Julienne the cheese into 1" pieces. In a covered pan, cook the potatoes in boiling water for 20 to 25 minutes, or until just tender, and drain. Peel and cut the potatoes into 1/4" cubes. In a very large bowl, combine the potatoes, bacon, cheese and onions. In a separate, medium bowl, combine the mayonnaise, cream, mustard and pepper; add to the potatoes. Toss to coat. Cover and chill for 6 to 24 hours.

PREP TIME: 20 minutes | **COOK TIME:** 25 minutes | **CHILL:** 6 to 24 hours | **SERVES:** 10

AZURE EGGPLANT

5 small eggplants, peeled and cut into small cubes

Salted water

1 medium onion, chopped

1 medium bell pepper, chopped

2 Tablespoons butter

2 to 3 Tablespoons cooking oil

1 1/4 pounds ground beef

2 cups cooked rice

Salt and pepper, to taste

Bread crumbs

Butter

Preheat the oven to 325°.

Soak the eggplants in salted water for 20 minutes. Drain. Sauté the onion, bell pepper and eggplant in butter and oil until tender and wilted. Add ground beef and cook until the meat is no longer red. Add the cooked rice, salt and pepper. Cook until the rice is hot and blended with other ingredients. Place the eggplant mixture in a casserole, sprinkle lightly with the bread crumbs and dot with the butter. Bake uncovered in the oven for 20 minutes.

PREP TIME: 20 minutes | **COOK TIME:** 1 hour 15 minutes | **SERVES:** 6 to 8

COMFORTING CREAMY POTATOES

2 pounds Russet potatoes

3 garlic cloves, minced

2 cups chicken stock

1/4 teaspoon white pepper

Salt, to taste

1/4 cup heavy cream

Chopped chives (optional)

Peel the potatoes and cut into 1/4" cubes. Place the potatoes in a heavy saucepan. Stir in the garlic, chicken stock, pepper and salt. Bring the mixture to a boil and stir. Reduce the heat to very low, cover, and simmer for 10 minutes, stirring occasionally. The potatoes are cooked when they are soft at the edges but still retain their shape. The broth should be creamy and thick. If not, stir the potatoes to give off more starch. Just before serving, stir the cream into the hot potato mixture. Heat briefly, just enough to warm. If desired, add more cream. You should end up with soft cubes of potatoes in a creamy, rich sauce. Garnish with a sprinkling of chives before serving (optional).

PREP TIME: 20 minutes | **COOK TIME:** 30 minutes | **SERVES:** 4 to 6

SPIKED SAUTÉED MUSHROOMS

1 Tablespoon butter
4 cups whole mushrooms
1/2 cup onion, chopped
1 teaspoon garlic salt
1/4 cup chicken broth
1/2 cup beef broth
1 cup Chablis wine

Heat the butter in a skillet until melted. Add the mushrooms and onions and cook until onions are tender. Add the garlic salt, both broths and wine. Simmer 15 minutes.

PREP TIME: 10 minutes | COOK TIME: 30 minutes | SERVES: 8

POTATO AND ONION PIE

2 Tablespoons butter

1 cup new potatoes, sliced 1/4" thick

1 medium onion, thinly sliced and separated into rings

1/4 cup parsley, chopped

1/4 cup milk

8 eggs, beaten

1 cup Swiss cheese, shredded

1/4 teaspoon salt

1/4 teaspoon pepper

1 medium ripe tomato, cut in 1/4" slices

Preheat the oven to 400°.

In a 10" ovenproof skillet, melt the butter in the oven for about 3 to 4 minutes. Add the potatoes and onion. Bake for 15 to 20 minutes, until crisp-tender, stirring once. In a large bowl, stir together the parsley, milk, eggs, Swiss cheese, salt and pepper. Pour the mixture over the potatoes and onion; arrange tomato slices over the top. Return to the oven and bake for 17 to 22 minutes until the eggs are set and lightly browned.

PREP TIME: 20 minutes | COOK TIME: 40 minutes | SERVES: 4

SHOOTING FOR 100% EFFICIENCY

by Kelly Powers

The common person might view a mallard pick up off the water, fly 200 yards, sit down at another location, and not think twice about it. The question that needs to be addressed is why did that duck leave? What did he prefer in that different spot? Where and how did it land in relation to other birds? If hunters become more observant to these occurrences, they will become more proficient in pursuing waterfowl. The main thing you should constantly shoot for is 100% efficiency. For example, if I see only ten bunches all day, then I want to generate shooting opportunities at all of them. If there is one bunch that does not want to work, I try to find out reasons why. I feel if a hunter puts himself in the right spot (directly under the birds' flight patterns) then he should be able to finish them. This may sound far-fetched, but establishing high goals will only supplement your efficiency level. The old saying "they just don't want to work today" doesn't sit well with me. I feel there is a reason for everything; indeed, most of the time, ducks and geese are observing intricacies unnoticeable to us. If every person develops the mentality and desire to become a more efficient hunter, anything is possible.

GREEN BEANS AND TOMATOES

3/4 pound green beans

1/2 cup red onion rings

1/4 cup Italian dressing

2 tomatoes, cut into thin wedges

2 Tablespoons fresh basil, chopped

Place the green beans, onion and dressing in a microwaveable bowl and cover. Microwave on high 8 to 10 minutes, or until the beans are crisp-tender, stirring after 2 minutes. Stir in the tomatoes and basil. Serve.

PREP TIME: 15 minutes | COOK TIME: 8 to 10 minutes | SERVES: 6

ROSEMARY GARLIC NEW POTATOES

1 large sprig fresh rosemary

12 ounces new potatoes

1 Tablespoon minced garlic in oil

1/4 teaspoon salt

1/4 teaspoon pepper

2 Tablespoons water

Preheat the oven to 375°.

Mix the rosemary, potatoes, garlic in oil, salt, pepper and water in a medium-size baking dish. Cover and bake in the oven for 30 minutes or until tender.

PREP TIME: 10 minutes | COOK TIME: 30 minutes | SERVES: 4

BROILED TOMATOES

4 medium ripe tomatoes, sliced

1/4 cup cracker crumbs

1/4 teaspoon salt

1/4 teaspoon dried oregano or basil

1/4 teaspoon dried thyme

1 Tablespoon oil

Parsley sprigs

Preheat the oven to broil.

Wash the tomatoes and slice in half crosswise. Place on a baking sheet, cut side up. Mix the crumbs, seasonings and oil. Sprinkle some of the mixture on each tomato. Broil 8 to 10 inches from the heat for about 4 minutes, or until golden brown. Garnish with parsley sprigs.

PREP TIME: 10 minutes | COOK TIME: 4 minutes | SERVES: 4

SCALLOPED PINEAPPLE

2 cups sugar

2 sticks margarine

3 eggs, beaten

1 (16 oz.) can crushed pineapple

4 cups white bread crumbs

Preheat the oven to 350°.

Cream the sugar and margarine together; add the eggs and mix well. Add the pineapple to the mixture, then the bread crumbs, and stir well. Bake in an ovenproof dish for 1 hour 15 minutes.

PREP TIME: 15 minutes | COOK TIME: 1 hour 15 minutes | SERVES: 12

BLACK BEANS AND RICE

1 teaspoon olive oil

1/4 cup onion, chopped

1/4 cup green bell pepper, chopped

3 garlic cloves, minced

2 cups black beans, cooked

1 cup black bean broth or water

2 Tablespoons brewed coffee

2 cups cooked rice, cooled

1 teaspoon Worcestershire

Salt and pepper

2 Tablespoons fresh cilantro, chopped

Heat the oil in a large, heavy skillet. Add the onion, bell pepper and garlic. Cook until the onion is translucent, stirring occasionally, about 10 minutes. Add the beans, broth and coffee. Simmer until slightly thickened, about 15 minutes. Add the rice, Worcestershire, salt and pepper. Simmer 5 minutes to blend flavors. Garnish with cilantro and serve.

PREP TIME: 15 minutes | **COOK TIME:** 35 to 40 minutes | **SERVES:** 4

JAMBALAYA GRITS

2 Tablespoons bacon grease
2 Tablespoons flour
1/2 cup onion, chopped
1 green pepper, chopped
1/2 cup celery, chopped
1 cup quick grits, uncooked
1 cup fresh tomatoes, peeled and chopped
1 cup ground ham
Cooked bacon

In a heavy skillet, heat the bacon grease and gradually add the flour, stirring constantly until the roux is light brown. Add the onion, green pepper and celery. Cook 5 minutes. Cook the grits according to the package directions and add to the roux, breaking up the grits if necessary. Add the tomatoes and ham. Sprinkle with the bacon and serve immediately.

PREP TIME: 20 minutes | **COOK TIME:** 20 minutes | **SERVES:** 6 to 8

DAVY'S SALSA ROJA

submitted by DAVY HITE

10 to 12 roma tomatoes
2 to 3 jalapenos
1/4 medium onion
3 Tablespoons sugar
1 teaspoon pressed garlic
1/2 to 1 teaspoon salt
1/4 to 1/2 teaspoon black pepper
Juice of 1/2 lime
Cilantro, to taste

Combine ingredients in food processor and chop to desired consistency. May be chopped by hand for a chunkier salsa. All ingredients may be adjusted to individual taste. Serve with tortilla chips.

PREP TIME: 20 minutes | SERVES: 12 to 15

HABITAT TIPS *by Davy Hite*

Whether you are hunting deer, turkey or other wild game in your neck of the woods, or fishing for trophy bass thousands of miles from home, you should always start by looking for two key elements: habitat or cover and food sources. Try to find the best habitat or cover available depending upon your particular location and time of year. Locating the best food sources for the object of your chase is also critical to a successful hunt or creel. If available, concentrate on food sources high in protein such as acorns or alfalfa for game and crawfish for bass.

EASY YAMS

4 to 5 fresh yams
Unsweetened apple juice
Butter or margarine (optional)
Cinnamon (optional)
Cloves (optional)
Nutmeg (optional)
1 (6 oz.) can apple juice concentrate

Peel, wash and cut the yams in chunks and put in a large pan. Cover the yams with the apple juice and bring to a boil. Cook until tender. Mash the yams, blending in the butter, cinnamon, cloves, nutmeg and apple juice concentrate to the desired consistency.

PREP TIME: 15 minutes | **COOK TIME:** 40 minutes | **SERVES:** 6 to 8

CAULIFLOWER PARMESAN

1 cauliflower head, separated into 12 florets

1 Tablespoon salt

1/4 cup bread crumbs

1/4 cup Parmesan cheese, grated

1 egg

1 Tablespoon milk

2 Tablespoons margarine, melted

Preheat the oven to 350°.

Cook the cauliflower for 7 minutes in salted water. Drain. Mix the bread crumbs with the cheese. Beat the egg with the milk. Dip each floret in the egg wash, then in the crumb mixture. Arrange the cauliflower in a buttered casserole. Pour the melted margarine over the cauliflower. Cover and bake in the oven for 20 minutes.

PREP TIME: 15 minutes | COOK TIME: 30 minutes | SERVES: 6

SOUPS

FISH NOODLE SOUP

2 medium carrots

1 celery rib

1 quart water

1 small onion, cut into thin wedges

1/4 cup fresh parsley, snipped

2 teaspoons instant chicken bouillon granules

1/2 teaspoon salt

1/4 teaspoon dried thyme leaves

1/8 teaspoon pepper

1/2 cup uncooked narrow egg noodles

1 cup cooked lean fish, flaked

Peel and cut the carrots into diagonal slices. Cut the celery into thin slices. In a 2-quart saucepan, combine the carrots, water, celery, onion, parsley, bouillon granules, salt, thyme and pepper. Heat to boiling. Reduce the heat, cover and simmer 10 minutes. Add the noodles and return to a boil. Cook until the noodles are tender, 8 to 10 minutes. Stir in the fish. Simmer for 1 minute.

PREP TIME: 20 minutes | **COOK TIME:** 30 minutes | **SERVES:** 4 to 6

PHEASANT SOUP

3 pheasant carcasses

Vegetable oil

1/2 cup onion, coarsely chopped

1/2 cup carrots, coarsely chopped

1/2 cup celery, coarsely chopped

Seasonings

Cornstarch (optional)

Noodles, rice, barley, vegetables or potatoes

Place the carcasses in a large stockpot with a small amount of vegetable oil and add the onions, carrots and celery. Brown thoroughly on high heat until the vegetables begin to caramelize and the meat is well done. (Undercooking will cause cloudy stock from blood cooked out of the meat into the stock.) The dark color of the caramelized vegetables makes a rich, dark stock, about the color of tea. Add water to cover and simmer until the meat can easily be removed from the bones. Take the bones out of the stock; strain the stock to remove the remaining vegetables and scraps. Season to taste. Remove the meat from the bones and reserve for the soup. If desired, add a small amount of cornstarch dissolved in water to give body to the stock. Cook noodles, rice, wild rice, barley, vegetables or potatoes in the stock. Add the meat at the last minute; heat through.

PREP TIME: 30 minutes | **COOK TIME:** 1 hour | **SERVES:** 6 to 8

DUTCH OVEN TURTLE SOUP

Meat from a 5- to 8-pound alligator, snapping or softshell turtle, cut in 1/2" cubes

Bacon drippings

6 large potatoes

1 onion

1 (1 pound) bag carrots

1 (16 oz.) can corn

1 (14 oz.) can beef or chicken stock

Brown the meat in the bacon drippings. Cut the vegetables into large chunks. Put all the turtle meat, potatoes, onion, carrots, corn and beef or chicken stock in a Dutch oven; cover with water. Bury the Dutch oven in a fire pit under coals. After 8 hours, dig out the pot and dig in.

PREP TIME: 20 minutes | **COOK TIME:** 8 1/2 hours | **SERVES:** 4 to 6

BEER CHEESE SOUP

8 cups milk

2 teaspoons Tabasco®

4 teaspoons Worcestershire

4 Tablespoons chicken stock

16 oz. Cheez Whiz®

6 Tablespoons cornstarch

1/3 cup water

1 cup beer

Cayenne pepper

Combine the milk, Tabasco®, Worcestershire and chicken stock. Bring to a boil, stirring regularly. Add the Cheez Whiz®, after warming the uncovered jar in hot water or in the microwave. Mix in well. Dissolve the cornstarch completely in the water and add to the soup, which should thicken immediately. Reduce the heat a bit and stir in the beer. To serve, ladle into bowls and dust with the cayenne pepper.

PREP TIME: 5 minutes | COOK TIME: 25 minutes | SERVES: 6

BECOME A METEOROLOGIST

by Kelly Powers

The start of each hunt should always rely on checking the weather forecast every morning. At our club, we have the use of a DTN radar screen. It really helps to have the current national weather conditions at our fingertips. Any slight change can significantly affect the flight patterns of waterfowl. On numerous occasions I have witnessed people leaving at 9 AM not knowing a major front will roll through around 10:30. At times such as these, hunting can be superb. So pay special attention to weather details and be sure to log your data for future reference.

DUCK SOUP

2 duck carcasses

3 onions, chopped

3 carrots, chopped

1 rib celery, chopped

6 pints water

Bouquet garni

Salt and pepper

4 oz. red wine

Parsley, chopped

Preheat the oven to 450°.

Remove all the skin and fat from the carcasses and reserve. Chop the carcasses into small pieces and put them into a roasting pan with 2 of the onions, the carrots and celery. Place in the oven and cook for 30 minutes, turning occasionally until brown all over. Remove the carcasses to a stockpot. Add the cold water, the bouquet garni, salt and pepper. Add the red wine to the roasting pan and stir over medium heat to loosen the sediment; add it to the stock pot. Bring the mixture to a boil, skim away any foam, and simmer for 4 to 5 hours, skimming the surface occasionally. Strain the stock into a fresh pot and reduce it to 1 1/2 pints. Cool and remove all fat. Add the remaining chopped vegetables and cook for 30 minutes. Sprinkle with chopped parsley and serve.

PREP TIME: 30 minutes | **COOK TIME:** 6 hours | **SERVES:** 10 to 12

ONION SOUP

1/2 pound white onions, sliced

1/4 cup butter

2 Tablespoons corn oil

3 Tablespoons all purpose flour

1 quart chicken broth

1 quart beef broth

8 slices French bread

Swiss cheese, shredded

Parmesan cheese, grated

Sauté the onions in butter and oil until onions are transparent, but not browned. When tender, turn the heat to the lowest point and sprinkle the onions with flour, stirring vigorously. Pour into a Dutch oven and stir in the broths. Heat thoroughly and divide among 8 ovenproof bowls.

Preheat broiler.

Float a slice of the bread atop each bowl of soup. Mix equal parts of the Swiss and the Parmesan cheeses to a smooth paste and spread over the bread. Place all the bowls on an oven rack 4" from the broiler and broil until the cheese melts. Serve at once.

PREP TIME: 20 minutes | **COOK TIME:** 30 minutes | **SERVES:** 6

SIMPLE CORN CHOWDER

2 medium potatoes, chopped

1 medium onion, chopped

2 cups water

1 (16 oz.) can creamed corn

1 (10 oz.) can corn niblets

1 cup milk

Salt and pepper

Butter

In a saucepan, cook the potatoes and onion in boiling water. Once cooked, do not drain the cooking liquid; add the cans of corn. Add the milk and salt and pepper, to taste. Continue heating until hot. Put a pat of butter in the soup bowl; ladle in the hot soup.

PREP TIME: 5 minutes | **COOK TIME:** 35 minutes | **SERVES:** 4

POTATO SOUP

1 1/2 cups potatoes, peeled and grated

2 Tablespoons onion, grated

1 (11 oz.) can evaporated milk

2 cups milk

1/4 cup water

2 Tablespoons all purpose flour

Salt and pepper

2 Tablespoons fresh parsley

Place the potatoes and onions in a saucepan and cover with water. Bring the water to a boil, reduce the heat to medium, and simmer until the potatoes are done. Do not drain. Add the evaporated milk and the regular milk. Continue cooking and stirring until the mixture is hot. Combine the water and flour and mix until blended and add to the potato mixture, stirring until mixture thickens. Add the salt and pepper to taste. Stir in the parsley.

PREP TIME: 30 minutes | **COOK TIME:** 50 minutes to 1 hour | **SERVES:** 4

VENISON SOUP

1/2 pound venison

1 onion, diced

2 carrots, diced

3 ribs celery, diced

6 pods okra, chopped

1 (15 oz.) can whole kernel corn

1 (15 oz.) can English peas

4 potatoes, peeled and diced

2 quarts tomatoes

Salt and pepper

Put the venison in a soup pot and cover with water; cook until tender. Take the meat out of the pan and chop. Add the onion, carrots and celery to the pot along with the chopped venison. Cook until vegetables are tender. Add the okra, corn, peas and potatoes to the pot and cook until potatoes are done. Add tomatoes and bring to a boil. Add salt and pepper to taste.

PREP TIME: 30 minutes | **COOK TIME:** 1 1/2 hours | **SERVES:** 4

VEGETABLE AND CHEESE CHOWDER

1/3 cup uncooked quick or old-fashioned oats

1 cup celery, sliced

1/2 cup onion, chopped

2 Tablespoons butter

2 cups milk

2 cups water

1 (16 oz.) package frozen mixed vegetables

1 teaspoon mustard

1/2 teaspoon salt

1/8 teaspoon black pepper

2 cups cheddar cheese, shredded

Place the oats in a food processor or blender, cover and process for 1 minute. In a 4-quart saucepan or a Dutch oven, sauté the celery and onion in the butter until tender. Blend in the ground oats. Gradually add the milk and water. Continue cooking over medium heat, stirring constantly, until thickened. Reduce the heat. Add the vegetables, mustard, salt and pepper. Continue cooking over low heat for 10 minutes, or until the vegetables are heated through. Remove from the heat, add the cheese and stir until well blended.

Note:

For the frozen vegetables, you can substitute canned or fresh vegetables of your choice, but you will need to cut the cooking time down a bit.

PREP TIME: 15 minutes | **COOK TIME:** 25 minutes | **SERVES:** 4 to 6

NEW ENGLAND CLAM CHOWDER

2 (6 oz.) cans clams, chopped

2 (10 1/2 oz.) cans condensed potato soup

1 cup half-and-half

1 medium onion, finely diced

2 garlic cloves, finely diced

Drain 1 can of the clams, but save the liquid from the remaining can. Mix the potato soup, clams, clams with liquid, half-and-half, onion and garlic into a medium saucepan and bring to a boil over medium heat, stirring constantly for 10 to 15 minutes. Reduce the heat to low and simmer for an additional 10 minutes.

PREP TIME: 15 minutes | **COOK TIME:** 20 to 30 minutes | **SERVES:** 4-6

SAUCES AND MARINADES

FISHING CRAPPIE

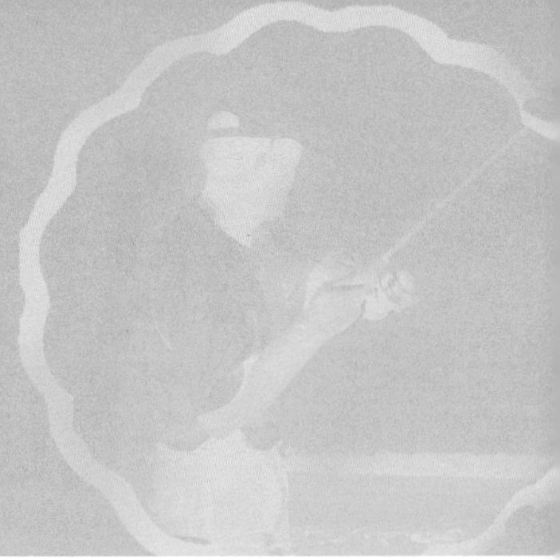

When fishing submerged cover, cast jigs and spinners beyond the potential crappie lair and let them sink to the desired level before beginning a slow, swimming retrieve. A 1/16 oz. jig sinks about 1 foot per second. If you are fishing a crappie bed in 12 feet of water and the stakes stick up 3 feet above the bottom, count the jig down 9 feet and fan cast the area. The crappie may hold off to the side of the bed, down in the bed or suspend somewhere above it. Vary the count until you begin getting strikes.

SIMPLE SAUCE

1 cup chili sauce

1 Tablespoon fresh lime or lemon juice

1/2 teaspoon prepared horseradish

In a small serving bowl, blend the chili sauce, lime juice and horseradish. Chill for at least 30 minutes to blend flavors.

PREP TIME: 10 minutes | CHILL TIME: 30 minutes | MAKES: 1 cup

WHITE SAUCE

2 Tablespoons butter

2 Tablespoons all purpose flour

1 cup milk

1/4 teaspoon salt

Dash of pepper (optional)

Melt the butter in a sauce pan and blend in the flour. Slowly add the milk, stirring constantly. Cook for 5 minutes. Add the salt and pepper.

Variation:

Depending on what you're serving with the white sauce, you can add other seasonings, such as paprika, herbal seasoning, garlic and onion. To make cream of mushroom soup, add mushrooms, garlic, extra pepper and a touch more milk. You can make other cream soups by adding chicken, turkey, roast beef, celery, peas ... you name it.

PREP TIME: 5 minutes | **COOK TIME:** 10 minutes | **MAKES:** 1 1/4 cups

BASIC TARTAR SAUCE

1/2 cup mayonnaise or salad dressing

1/8 teaspoon salt

2 Tablespoons chopped sweet pickle relish

2 Tablespoons sour cream

2 Tablespoons fresh lime or lemon juice

2 Tablespoons onion, finely chopped

Dash curry powder (optional)

Mix the mayonnaise, salt, pickle relish, sour cream, lime juice, onion and curry powder in a small bowl. Chill for at least 30 minutes to blend flavors.

PREP TIME: 10 minutes | **CHILL TIME:** 30 minutes | **MAKES:** 1 1/2 cups

HOT TARTAR SAUCE

1 cup mayonnaise

1 teaspoon Dijon mustard

1 teaspoon finely grated lemon zest

1 Tablespoon fresh lemon juice

Dash of Tabasco®

2 Tablespoons drained sweet pickle relish

2 Tablespoons flat-leaf parsley, chopped

2 Tablespoons shallots, finely minced

1 Tablespoon tiny capers, drained

Salt

Black pepper, freshly ground

Combine the mayonnaise, mustard, lemon zest, lemon juice, Tabasco® and relish in a bowl. Stir in the remaining ingredients. Refrigerate, covered, at least 1 hour before serving to allow flavors to blend. Store refrigerated; it will last up to 3 days.

PREP TIME: 15 minutes | **CHILL TIME:** 1 hour | **MAKES:** 2 cups

HUNTING DOVE

In late afternoon when the temperature is the warmest, doves will seek water before roosting for the evening. Set up your blind around a source of water and be well camouflaged for when the action heats up.

TANGY HERB SAUCE

3/4 cup sour cream

3 Tablespoons Dijon mustard

1 teaspoon basil

1/2 teaspoon onion powder

2 Tablespoons parsley, finely chopped

Mix the sour cream, mustard, basil, onion powder and parsley well. Serve over fish.

PREP TIME: 10 minutes | MAKES: 1 cup

BASIC PAN GRAVY

Pan drippings from a wild turkey

Melted unsalted butter (if needed)

About 4 cups turkey stock or broth

3/4 cup all purpose flour

1/3 cup bourbon, port or dry sherry (optional)

Pour the drippings from the roasting pan into a heat-proof glass bowl or large measuring cup. Let stand for 5 minutes and then skim off and reserve the fat that rises to the top. Measure out 3/4 cup of the fat, adding the melted butter, if needed. Add enough turkey stock to the skimmed pan drippings to make 6 cups total. Place the roasting pan over low heat on two burners of the stove and add the skimmed fat. Whisk in the flour, scraping up the browned bits on the bottom of the pan. Cook until lightly browned, about 2 minutes. Whisk in the pan drippings mixture and bourbon, or other liquor, if desired. Cook, whisking often, until the gravy has thickened and is lump-free, about 5 minutes. Transfer to a warmed gravy boat and serve.

PREP TIME: 10 minutes | **COOK TIME:** 15 minutes | **MAKES:** about 6 cups

DUCK BASTE

1/4 cup honey

1/2 cup soy sauce

1/2 cup sherry

1 garlic clove, finely minced

1 teaspoon freshly grated gingerroot, or 1/2 teaspoon ground ginger

Combine the honey, soy sauce, sherry, garlic and ginger in a saucepan; bring to a boil and remove from the heat. Use the sauce to baste a duck every 15 minutes as it roasts or turns on the spit.

PREP TIME: 10 minutes | MAKES: 1 1/4 cups

BROWN GRAVY

2 1/2 Tablespoons solid vegetable oil
4 Tablespoons flour
1 Tablespoon onion, chopped
1 small tomato
2 cups vegetable broth or water
Salt

Put the oil in a frying pan and, when hot, add the flour and stir constantly until brown. Add the chopped onion and continue to stir for a few minutes. Add the tomato and stir for 5 minutes or until the liquid is almost evaporated (this will give the gravy a good flavor). Add a third of the broth or water and stir until smooth and free from lumps. Add the rest of the liquid and let boil slowly for 10 minutes. Strain and serve.

PREP TIME: 10 minutes | **COOK TIME:** 30 minutes | **MAKES:** about 2 cups

HUNTING DUCK

If you expect the wind to change while you're hunting, try putting out three or four groups of decoys to cover any possible wind change and keep yourself from having to move decoys while the birds are flying.

LEMON PARSLEY SAUCE

1/2 stick butter, melted

3 Tablespoons lemon juice

1 teaspoon lemon peel, grated

1 Tablespoon parsley, chopped

Melt the butter and add the lemon juice, lemon peel and parsley. Mix well.

PREP TIME: 15 minutes | **MAKES:** 1 cup

GIBLET GRAVY

Giblets and neck of wild fowl

2 Tablespoons chicken fat

2 Tablespoons all purpose flour

Salt and pepper

Place the giblets (liver, heart and gizzard) and the neck in a saucepan and cover them with cold water. Simmer slowly and, when the giblets are tender, remove the meat from the neck and finely chop with the giblets, saving the water in which they were cooked. Heat the fat on top of the stove and stir in the flour. Cook 2 minutes; then add 1 cup of the stock left from cooking the giblets, pouring it in gradually so as not to thin the gravy too much. (If the gravy seems too thick, add a little hot water.) Put in the chopped giblets and season to taste with salt and pepper.

PREP TIME: 10 minutes | **COOK TIME:** 15 minutes | **MAKES:** about 1 1/2 cups

RED WINE MARINADE

2 cups dry red wine

1 bunch scallions, sliced

1 clove garlic, minced

1/2 cup olive oil

1/4 cup soy or teriyaki sauce

2 Tablespoons dark brown sugar

1 teaspoon fresh ginger, grated

1 Tablespoon Worcestershire

Mix the wine, scallions, garlic, olive oil, soy sauce, brown sugar, ginger and Worcestershire. Use the mixture for a marinade, or boil it for 10 minutes to use as a basting sauce.

PREP TIME: 20 minutes | **COOK TIME:** 10 minutes | **MAKES:** about 3 cups

WILD GAME MARINADE

6 Tablespoons lemon juice

2 teaspoons salt

1/2 cup water

1/2 teaspoon pepper

1/2 cup ketchup

2 onions, sliced (optional)

1 teaspoon chili powder

1 garlic clove, minced

Mix the lemon juice, salt, water, pepper, ketchup, onions, chili powder and garlic. Use the mixture for a marinade or basting.

PREP TIME: 15 minutes | **MAKES:** about 2 cups

SHERRY MARINADE

1 package dry Italian dressing

1 cup cooking sherry

1/2 cup oil

1/4 cup soy sauce

1/4 cup Worcestershire

1 large onion, diced

Mix the Italian dressing, sherry, oil, soy sauce, Worcestershire and onion in a medium bowl.

PREP TIME: 15 minutes | **MAKES:** about 3 cups

ASIAN STYLE MARINADE

1/2 cup soy sauce

1/2 cup onions, minced

2 Tablespoons sesame seeds

2 Tablespoons salad oil

2 teaspoons salt

2 Tablespoons light brown sugar

2 teaspoons lemon juice

1/2 teaspoon pepper

1/2 teaspoon ginger

Combine the soy sauce, onions, sesame seeds, salad oil, salt, sugar, lemon juice, pepper and ginger in a medium bowl.

PREP TIME: 20 minutes | COOK TIME: 10 minutes | MAKES: about 3 cups

SPICY–HOT MARINADE

4 green onions

2 jalapeños or serranos, seeded

1/3 cup lemon juice

1/4 cup honey

2 Tablespoons vegetable oil

2 Tablespoons fresh thyme leaves, or 2 teaspoons dried thyme

1/2 teaspoon salt

1/4 teaspoon ground allspice

1/4 teaspoon nutmeg

Place the onions, jalapeños, lemon juice, honey, vegetable oil, thyme, salt, allspice and nutmeg in a food processor or blender and blend until smooth.

PREP TIME: 20 minutes | **MAKES:** about 1 cup

DESSERTS

BREAD PUDDING

10 slices bread

3 cups skim milk

1 1/2 cups sugar

1 cup egg substitute

4 Tablespoons diet margarine

2 teaspoons vanilla extract

1 cup crushed pineapple

Preheat the oven to 350°.

Break the bread into pieces and place in a 9 x 13" baking dish. Blend in half the milk. Add the sugar and egg substitute, mixing well after each. Dice the margarine on top and stir in the vanilla, remaining milk and pineapple. Bake for 40 minutes, until firm.

PREP TIME: 10 minutes | **COOK TIME:** 40 minutes | **SERVES:** 6 to 8

PERSIMMON PUDDING

1 pint buttermilk
1 pint ripe persimmons
1 cup sugar
1 egg
1 Tablespoon butter
1/2 teaspoon baking powder
1/2 teaspoon baking soda
1/4 teaspoon cloves
1/2 teaspoon allspice
1 teaspoon cinnamon
Flour for a thin batter
Topping (recipe follows)

Preheat the oven to 350°.

Mix the buttermilk with the persimmons. Press through a sieve or colander; add the sugar, egg, butter, baking powder, baking soda, cloves, allspice and cinnamon. Add enough flour to make a stiff batter, but not as stiff as cake dough. Bake in a square pan at 350°, until done. When you are ready to serve, cut the pudding into squares. Place the squares on a broiler pan and spoon the topping over the squares. Turn the oven to broil and place the squares under the broiler; cook until bubbly.

TOPPING

1/2 cup sugar
1/4 cup milk
1/2 teaspoon cinnamon
1 Tablespoon flour
1 Tablespoon butter

Mix the sugar, milk, cinnamon and flour. Bring to a boil. Add the butter; stir to combine.

Note:

If the pudding falls a little, so much the better. And if it seems soggy, that's also for the better.

PREP TIME: 15 minutes | **COOK TIME:** 40 minutes | **SERVES:** 6 to 8

CHOCOLATE CHESS PIE

1/2 stick margarine

3 Tablespoons cocoa

1 1/2 cups sugar

1/2 cup chopped pecans

1 teaspoon flour

2 eggs, slightly beaten

1 teaspoon vanilla

1/2 cup evaporated milk

1 9" piecrust, unbaked

Preheat the oven to 400°.

Melt the margarine. Add the cocoa, sugar, pecans, flour, eggs, vanilla and evaporated milk; mix thoroughly. Pour into the piecrust. Bake in the oven for 10 minutes. Reduce the oven temperature to 325°, and bake for 30 minutes more.

PREP TIME: 20 minutes | **COOK TIME:** 40 minutes | **SERVES:** 8

FROZEN SALAD OR DESSERT

1 (8 oz.) package cream cheese, softened

1 (8 oz.) bowl refrigerated whipped topping

1 (10 oz.) package strawberries

1 cup pecans or walnuts, chopped

1 (20 oz.) can crushed pineapple, with juice

3/4 cup sugar

3 bananas

Mix the cream cheese well with the whipped topping; add the strawberries nuts, pineapple, sugar, and bananas. Pour into a freezer container and freeze. The dessert will keep for several weeks.

PREP TIME: 20 minutes | **SERVES:** 6 to 8

CHESS FRUIT PIE

1 cup brown sugar

1/2 cup margarine

1/2 cup cream

3 whole eggs

1 egg yolk

1 cup English walnuts, chopped

1 cup raisins

1 teaspoon vanilla

1 teaspoon lemon peel

1 teaspoon lemon juice

2 Tablespoons white sugar

1 egg white, stiffly beaten

1 9" piecrust, unbaked

Whipping cream

Preheat the oven to 350°.

Combine the sugar and margarine. Add the cream and mix well. Add the eggs and yolk, one at a time, beating well after each addition. Add the nuts, raisins, vanilla, lemon peel and lemon juice. Mix well. Beat the white sugar into the stiffly beaten egg white and fold into the pie mixture. Pour into the piecrust and bake in the oven for 40 minutes or until set. Serve with a dollop of whipped cream.

PREP TIME: 20 minutes | **COOK TIME:** 40 minutes | **SERVES:** 8

FISHING RED SNAPPER

Snapper are also known to feed at selective depths that must be determined to highly be productive. They prefer the bottom of moderate depths, anywhere from about 60 to 400 feet, with the older populations of larger fish preferring the cooler water of deeper spots.

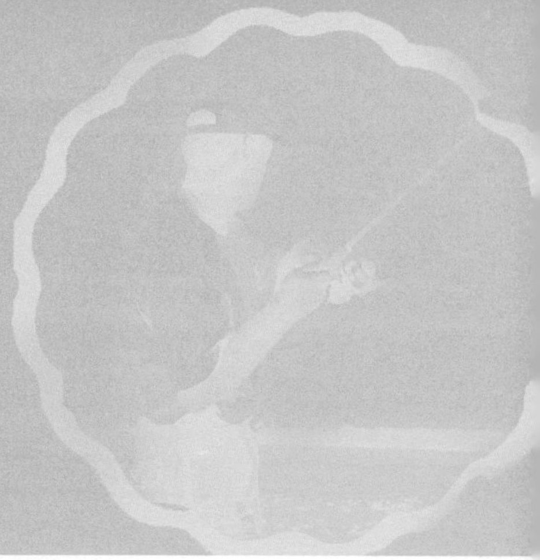

COCONUT PIE

2 eggs, beaten

1 cup milk

1/2 teaspoon vanilla extract

1/4 stick butter or margarine

1 cup sugar

1/4 cup self-rising flour

1 (3 1/2 oz.) package flaked coconut

Preheat the oven to 350°.

Beat the eggs. Blend in the milk, vanilla, butter, sugar, flour and coconut. Turn into a greased 9" pie pan. Bake in the oven for 30 minutes. The pie makes its own crust.

PREP TIME: 10 minutes | **COOK TIME:** 30 minutes | **SERVES:** 8

GRANNY'S EGG CUSTARD PIE

3 eggs

1 cup sugar

1/2 teaspoon salt

1/2 teaspoon vanilla extract

1/2 teaspoon nutmeg

1 pint milk, scalded

1 9" piecrust, unbaked

Preheat the oven to 325°.

Beat the eggs and add the sugar, salt, vanilla and nutmeg. Add the scalded (not boiled) milk and mix. Pour into the piecrust and bake in the oven for 50 minutes, or until a knife blade comes out clean.

PREP TIME: 10 minutes | COOK TIME: 50 minutes | SERVES: 8

APRICOT NECTAR CAKE

4 eggs

1 cup apricot nectar

3/4 cup oil

1 box lemon cake mix

Icing (recipe follows)

Preheat the oven to 350°.

Beat the eggs, apricot nectar and oil. Add the cake mix and beat again. Pour into a deep cake pan and bake in the oven for 40 minutes. Cool the cake and drizzle the icing over it.

ICING

1 cup powdered sugar

3 Tablespoons lemon juice

In a small bowl mix the sugar and lemon juice. Drizzle over cake before serving.

PREP TIME: 10 minutes | **COOK TIME:** 40 minutes | **SERVES:** 8

PECAN BARS

2 cups all purpose flour

1/2 cup sugar

1/8 teaspoon salt

3/4 cup (1 1/2 sticks) butter or margarine, plus 1/2 cup

1 cup brown sugar, firmly packed

1 cup light corn syrup

4 large eggs, lightly beaten

2 1/2 cups pecans, finely chopped

1 teaspoon vanilla extract

Preheat the oven to 350°.

Combine the flour, sugar and salt in a large bowl and cut in the 3/4 cup butter with a pastry blender until the mixture resembles very fine crumbs. Press the mixture evenly into a greased 13 x 9" pan, using a piece of plastic wrap to press the crumb mixture firmly in the pan. Bake in the oven for 17 to 20 minutes, or until lightly browned. Combine the brown sugar, corn syrup and the 1/2 cup butter in a saucepan; bring to a boil over medium heat, stirring gently. Remove from the heat. Stir 1/4 of the hot mixture into the beaten eggs and add to the remaining hot mixture. Stir in the pecans and vanilla. Pour the filling over the crust. Bake in the oven for 35 minutes, or until set. Cool completely in the pan on a wire rack. Cut into bars.

PREP TIME: 15 minutes | **COOK TIME:** 35 to 40 minutes | **YIELDS:** 28 to 30 (2-inch square) bars

LEMON CHESS PIE

2 cups sugar

1 Tablespoon flour

1 Tablespoon cornmeal

1/4 teaspoon salt

1/4 cup melted butter or margarine

1/4 cup lemon juice

Grated peel of 2 lemons

1/4 cup milk

4 eggs

1 9" piecrust, unbaked

Preheat the oven to 350°.

Combine the sugar, flour, cornmeal and salt. Add the butter, lemon juice, lemon peel and milk. Blend well. Add the eggs, beating well. Pour into the piecrust. Bake in the oven for 50 minutes.

PREP TIME: 10 minutes | **COOK TIME:** 50 minutes | **SERVES:** 8

BANANAS FOSTER

submitted by CLARK BRENNAN

1/4 cup butter
1 cup brown sugar
1/2 teaspoon cinnamon
1/4 cup banana liqueur
4 bananas, cut in half lengthwise, then halved
1/4 cup white rum
4 scoops vanilla ice cream

Combine the butter, sugar and cinnamon in a flambé pan or skillet. Place the pan over low heat, either on an alcohol burner or on top of the stove, and cook, stirring until the sugar dissolves. Stir in the banana liqueur, then place the bananas in the pan. When the banana sections soften and begin to brown, carefully add the rum. Continue to cook the sauce until the rum is hot, then tip the pan slightly to ignite the rum. When the flames subside, lift the bananas out of the pan and place four pieces over each portion of ice cream. Generously spoon warm sauce over the top of the ice cream and serve immediately.

PREP TIME: 10 minutes | COOK TIME: 25 minutes | SERVES: 4

TRITON BOATS

Our Recipe for Success

Just as a great recipe has many ingredients, Triton Boats has become a leader in fishing boats by offering the boating industry's most diverse product lineup. Most boat companies are content to build one or two styles of boats, but Triton offers a remarkable array of boats for all kinds of fishing, in both fiberglass and aluminum: bass, crappie, walleye, redfish and other saltwater species, even catfish. We don't ignore hunters, either; our duck boats are popular with waterfowl hunters nationwide.

Innovation is another ingredient of our success. Triton listens to fishermen and hunters, and we use their input to create exciting new models. Like our totally new line of fiberglass and aluminum walleye boats from 17 to 21 feet. Our new Light Tackle Series saltwater boats, a smash hit on the redfish tournament trail. Our new aluminum crappie boats. And our new X Series bass boats, featuring the award-winning Res-Q concealed boarding ladder.

Just as it takes quality ingredients and the right cooking techniques to prepare a great fish or game recipe, it takes the finest materials and proven construction methods to make a great fishing boat. Triton's fiberglass boats feature our exclusive Tri-Core composite construction. Our aluminum boats are built with premium 5052 stock and feature all-welded construction. And whether you choose fiberglass or aluminum, you get the confidence of knowing there's never any wood in a Triton boat.

Just as many great recipes have a secret ingredient, ours is the pride of ownership you get when you buy a Triton boat ... pride that comes with knowing you've chosen the finest fishing or hunting boat available.

Because we believe responsibly enjoying fish and game as table fare is an important part of the outdoor experience, we've compiled these recipes especially for Triton owners to share with their families and friends. Here's hoping you enjoy them!

EVINRUDE & JOHNSON

Bombardier, Experience the Extraordinary.

Bombardier has a tradition of making extraordinary ideas come to life. Ever since J.A. Bombardier founded the company in 1942, the name has been synonymous with quality and creativity. His pioneering spirit is a legacy that has kept us growing and exploring new frontiers.

At Bombardier Recreational Products, innovation and passion are at the heart of our commitment, our products and our brands. These values, which come alive through technology and design, have but one compelling purpose: to deliver to consumers the most extraordinary recreational experience anywhere.

In October 2003, Bombardier released to commerce its new Evinrude E-TEC™ outboard engine technology.

Evinrude E-TEC™ is the first Evinrude outboard designed with the full commitment of the world-class Bombardier team. And the outboard engine world will never be the same.

Evinrude E-TEC was built from the ground up by first studying what consumers want in an outboard, and then building an engine to match their needs. The result: Extraordinary new performance. No annoying "break-in" period. It's full throttle right out of the box. Three years of normal recreational use without any scheduled dealer maintenance, and that includes oil changes. An easy at-home winterization program. And don't forget, Evinrude E-TEC meets CARB 3-star emissions - a high mark in environmentally responsible performance for outboard motors.

Durability, Quality, Reliability. These three words are our mantra at Bombardier, and Evinrude E-TEC engines give you all three, thanks in part to oversized motor components throughout. Many of our V-6 engine parts are in E-TEC™ engines. They're not just big - they're space age. The pistons are made of a material we developed together with NASA. These pistons are more than twice as strong as ordinary pistons. Your E-TEC™ will be with you well into the future.

Available this year in 40, 50, 75 and 90 hp, an Evinrude E-TEC on your Triton boat gives a peace of mind that you're meeting the highest standards in quality boating, performance and reliability. But best of all, it gives you more time to create memories.

Bombardier Recreational Products designs, develops, builds, distributes and markets utility vehicles, Rotax™ engines and karts, Ski-Doo® and Lynx® snowmobiles, Bombardier™ ATVs, Sea-Doo® watercraft and sport boats, Johnson® and Evinrude® outboard engines, as well as Evinrude direct injection and Evinrude E-TEC™ technologies.

DELTA WATERFOWL

Dedicated to the Future of Waterfowl and Waterfowl Hunting

When James Ford Bell founded Delta Waterfowl in 1911, his goal was to put two ducks back for every bird harvested at his Delta Marsh duck camp in southern Manitoba.

During the drought of the 1930s Bell's concern for the waning resource prompted him to establish Delta's graduate research program, which was initiated by Hans Albert Hochbaum in 1938 under the supervision and mentorship of Aldo Leopold.

To date, Delta's student program has produced some 350 alumnus who have written more than 700 research papers. These volumes of valuable research contributed by these students have greatly enhanced our understanding of waterfowl and waterfowl management.

Graduates of Delta's student research program have gone on to pursue careers in wildlife and waterfowl management with the United States Fish and Wildlife Service and Canadian Wildlife Service, state and provincial agencies and private conservation organizations.

Research is still at the core of Delta's focus, but in recent years the organization has evolved into other areas of influence such as land-use and agricultural policy.

In addition to its original headquarters on Manitoba's famous Delta Marsh, Delta has added a United States office in Bismarck, North Dakota, in the heart of "the duck factory."

In 2003, the organization took a bold step launching its Delta Duck Production Program, an effort to apply direct management tools like predator control and nesting structures in areas where habitat alone isn't enough to increase production.

Delta strongly believes that waterfowl managers have a responsibility to "follow the science" when making management decisions. More than six decades of scientific discovery have shown that habitat projects scattered across a fragmented landscape are often not enough to boost duck production to population-expanding levels.

Research conducted by Hochbaum in the 1940s showed that nesting ducks need an abundance of seasonal and temporary wetlands in order to be successful. Most recently, science has shown that ducks need large blocks of grass nesting cover—40 percent of the landscape—in order to achieve population-expanding nest success.

Other research projects have demonstrated that nest success across the prairie pothole region (PPR) dropped dramatically from the 1930s to the 1990s, and that predation by an ever-increasing population of nest-raiding mammals like fox, raccoon and skunk is the single biggest factor inhibiting the growth of the duck population.

Delta believes waterfowl management must listen to the science and apply whatever tools are necessary to increase duck production. Two of the most viable tools currently at our disposal are predator management and Hen Houses (artificial nest structures).

Delta has been managing predators across the PPR for a decade with impressive results. When nest success predator blocks are compared to results from similar untapped areas, nest success is consistently two to three times higher on managed sites than on the "control blocks." In recent years Delta has expanded its efforts to include 36-square mile tracts, proving that large-scale predator management is effective.

Hen Houses also have proven to consistently increase nest success for mallards. With 80-percent usage rates and up to 80-percent nest success, Hen Houses are one of the most cost-effective tools for increasing production at management's disposal.

Delta Waterfowl also is committed to securing the future of waterfowl hunting through advocacy, public-policy work and involvement with youth programs. All of these efforts are done with a single guiding vision—to secure the future of waterfowl and waterfowl hunting.

A growing number of duck hunters have recognized the importance of the work being conducted by Delta and have thrown their support behind the organization. Membership has grown dramatically in recent years, allowing Delta to expand its on-the-ground programs and increase its research effort.

"Everyone associated with Delta Waterfowl is proud of the organization's journey of scientific discovery, from Al Hochbaum in the 1930s to the talented students working in the field today," says President Jonathan Scarth. "We're committed to continuing our legacy by putting that research to work producing more ducks for duck hunters."

Delta Waterfowl—doing good things for ducks.

For more information, visit our web site at **www.deltawaterfowl.org** or give us a call at 888-987-3695.

INDEX

Numbers in bold refer to pages with illustrations.

D

E

Q

R

S

U

V

W

X

Y

Z